COUGAR MANAGEMENT

D0597744

First Edition

THE COUGAR FUND

P.O. Box 122
JACKSON, WY 83001

Protecting America's Greatest Cat

Cougar Management Guidelines

First Edition

by the
Cougar Management Guidelines Working Group:

Tom Beck
John Beecham
Paul Beier
Terry Hofstra
Maurice Hornocker
Fred Lindzey
Kenneth Logan
Becky Pierce
Howard Quigley
Ian Ross
Harley Shaw
Rollin Sparrowe
Steve Torres

WildFutures
Bainbridge Island, Washington
2005

WildFutures
(206) 780-9718
cougar.guide@gmail.com

Library of Congress Control Number: 2005928358

ISBN-13:   978-0-9770075-0-9
ISBN-10:   0-9770075-0-2

The *Cougar Management Guidelines* are available for
$21.95 U.S./$28.95 Canadian, including shipping and
handling. Contact for quantity discounts.

Ordering Options:
Phone: (866) 375-9015
Email: orders@opalcreekpress.com
Fax: 503-363-6228
Mail: Opal Creek Press, LLC
             1675 Fir Street S.
             Salem, OR 97302
Visit us at www.opalcreekpress.com

Cover illustration © Dougald Stermer
Design and layout by Lorna Bernard

The text for this book is printed on 100% post-consumer chlorine free New Leaf paper.
The cover is printed on 15% post-consumer fiber.

For Ian Ross
1958 - 2003

Contents

ACKNOWLEDGEMENTS

This project was made possible through the generous support of the following foundations:
The Summerlee Foundation
Wilburforce Foundation
Margaret T. Morris Foundation
McCune Foundation
Norcross Wildlife Foundation
The William H. and Mattie Harris Foundation

We would like to acknowledge the following individuals and agencies for reviewing and making recommendations on the draft Cougar Management Guidelines. Some of the associations are listed for identification purposes only.

Rex Amack
Director
Nebraska Game and Parks Commission

William F. Andelt
Professor
Department of Fishery and Wildlife Biology
Colorado State University

Chuck Anderson
Trophy Game Section
Wyoming Game and Fish Department

Matt Austin
Large Carnivore Specialist
British Columbia Ministry of Water,
    Land and Air Protection

Michael E. Berger
Director, Wildlife Division
Texas Parks and Wildlife

Dave Brittell
Assistant Director, Wildlife Program
Washington Department of Fish and Wildlife

Eldon Burns
South West Regional Head, Wildlife
Fish and Wildlife Division
Sustainable Resource Development
Alberta, Canada

Terry Cleveland
Director
Wyoming Game and Fish Department

Robert L. Cook
Executive Director
Texas Parks and Wildlife

Craig Coolahan
California State Director
Wildlife Services
United States Department of Agriculture

Deanna Dawn
Wildlife Biologist
Live Oak Associates
San Jose, California

Melissa Grigione
Assistant Professor
Department of Environmental Science & Policy
University of South Florida

Rick Hopkins
Principal and Senior Wildlife Ecologist
Live Oak Associates
San Jose, California

Jonathan A. Jenks
Professor
Department of Wildlife and Fisheries Sciences
South Dakota State University

ACKNOWLEDGEMENTS (CONTINUED)

Gary M. Koehler
Principal Investigator
Project CAT (Cougars and Teaching)
Washington Department of Fish and Wildlife

Jeff Koenings
Director
Washington Department of Fish and Wildlife

David Mattson
Research Wildlife Biologist
USGS Southwest Biological Service Center
Northern Arizona University

Dave Moody
Trophy Game Biologist
Wyoming Game and Fish Department

Miles Moretti
Deputy Director
Utah Department of Natural Resources

Craig Moritmore
Interim Game Bureau Chief
Nevada Department of Wildlife

Kerry Murphy
Wildlife Biologist
Yellowstone Center for Resources
Yellowstone National Park, Wyoming

Chris Papouchis
Conservation Biologist
Mountain Lion Foundation

Alan Peoples
Chief of Wildlife
Oklahoma Game and Fish Department

Duane L. Shroufe
Director
Arizona Game and Fish Department

Bruce C. Thompson
Director
New Mexico Department of Game and Fish

James Unsworth
Chief
Bureau of Wildlife
Idaho Fish and Game

Doug Updike
Senior Wildlife Biologist
California Department of Fish and Game

Becky Weed
Rancher
13 Mile Lamb and Wool Company

Donald G. Whittaker
Assistant Staff Biologist, Big Game
Oregon Department of Fish and Wildlife

Russel Woolstenhulme
Staff Biologist
Nevada Department of Wildlife

Special Thanks

In addition to the reviewers, the Cougar Management Guidelines Working Group would like to thank the Western Association of Fish and Wildlife Agencies (WAFWA) which contributed by reviewing and making suggestions to the document. We would like to especially thank Larry Kruckenbery, WAFWA Executive Secretary, and Jim Unsworth for their assistance with WAFWA.

The Group would also like to thank Linda Sweanor, Cougar Ecologist, and Patricia M. Woodruff, Natural Resource Planner and Publisher, for their technical and editorial assistance, and Dougald Stermer for his artistic design of the cover.

PREFACE

The need for cougar (*Puma concolor*) management guidelines was conceived during the Sixth Mountain Lion Workshop at San Antonio, Texas with the realization that the body of cougar management and research literature had grown to the point that agencies and stakeholders alike were having difficulty keeping up with current knowledge.

Maurice Hornocker and his students at the University of Idaho carried out initial cougar research efforts in the 1960s. Following their lead, researchers in Arizona, Nevada, Utah, New Mexico, and California rapidly developed studies during the 1970s. The 1980s saw only a gradual increase in the number of cougar studies, allowing most managers to keep apace of new knowledge. However, research at various levels has now been carried out in virtually every western state and province in the United States and Canada, and is underway in Mexico and South America. Where a paucity of solid data regarding cougars existed prior to 1965, a plethora of information now exists.

As the body of scientific information about cougars grows, so do the challenges facing wildlife managers. In 1970, managers were primarily concerned with counting cougars and assessing their impacts on wild and domestic prey. Then, in the early 1990s, several cougar attacks on humans—including fatal attacks—added a new imperative for wildlife managers: developing strategies for managing cougar-human conflicts. By the late 1990s wildlife ecologists recognized that the greatest future challenge facing agencies would be minimizing the impact of habitat loss and fragmentation on cougar populations in the face of ever expanding human development in cougar habitat. This has increased concerns about the long-term compatibility of substantially increasing cougar harvests with conservation goals.

To assist wildlife managers, some medium is needed to synthesize the most current information into a form that can be easily translated into cougar management programs. The best models for such a process seem to be the management guidelines that have been developed for other species, including pronghorn (*Antilocapra americana*) and bighorn sheep (*Ovis canadensis*). Those of us in the first Cougar Management Guidelines Working Group have used those models to create this document. We view it as the beginning of a process, rather than a completed project.

We acknowledge that gaps exist in the guidelines due either to lack of reliable scientific information or to our own failure to incorporate available data. We hope the problem lies more in the former than the latter, and we have attempted to identify those areas where scientific information is lacking.

Our intent is that publication of these guidelines will be accompanied by the establishment of a continuing working group that will interact with wildlife agencies and other interested parties to initiate the next revision. To aid in this revision process, comments and suggestions for the maintenance and/or revision of this current document can be submitted electronically to cougar.guide@gmail.com. The composition of the next cougar guidelines working group is important. We attempted to select the best possible expertise, and variety of perspectives within our initial working group. We strongly recommend that the same thought and energy be expanded for the next group. These individuals should be recruited from state and federal governments, universities, and non-government organizations.

We believe that this document will make a substantial contribution to the management and conservation of cougars.

Harley Shaw   **Maurice Hornocker**

EXECUTIVE SUMMARY

The *Cougar Management Guidelines* were the result of an effort that was first initiated at a facilitated meeting in Boise, Idaho in October, 2002. The participants shared a common desire to benefit cougar conservation through developing guidelines that would integrate the history, most current research and methodologies, policies, and approaches to cougar conservation. The contributors to these guidelines included scientists from both academia and wildlife management agencies who have numerous publications and decades of experience in cougar conservation. They have volunteered their time for this initial effort, and they view these guidelines as a "living document" that will be maintained, updated, and rewritten as new information dictates.

The preparation of these guidelines proceeded with a team approach where individuals wrote select chapters that were later edited and rewritten by other members of the team. All members reviewed and edited all chapters, and agreed on a consistent format. In September 2004, the first complete draft was sent to select agency and university scientists for peer review. After incorporating numerous edits, the second draft was sent to all wildlife agencies in the western United States and Canada for their review and input. This version reflects changes made in light of agency comments. The authors hope that these guidelines will serve as a framework to help management agencies develop regional approaches toward the conservation of cougars and their habitat. The intended target audience for these guidelines is agency wildlife managers in Canada, the western United States, and Mexico.

These guidelines are organized into chapters that highlight the key facets of cougar conservation. Each chapter follows a similar format in which our major findings or recommendations are presented as numbered headings, followed by supporting information and references. The first chapter discusses the need for these guidelines, provides a historical perspective on cougar management and policies, and identifies an approach that considers: 1) conserving large landscapes for habitat connectivity, population viability, and regional management;

2) basing management strategies on the most reliable and current science; and 3) adopting an adaptive management approach toward addressing unknowns, assumptions, and effects of management prescriptions.

The remaining chapters in the *Cougar Management Guidelines* reference important information about: 1) predator and prey relationships and the need for cougar management with respect to prey populations; 2) the importance and utility of mapping cougar habitat for identifying important habitat features and defining cougar populations; 3) considering metapopulation and source-sink structure for defining cougar populations over broad regions; 4) methodologies and approaches to monitoring and assessing cougar populations; 5) depredation conflicts and the importance of identification, education, and data collection protocols; 6) considering large landscapes and zone management approaches for cougar harvest strategies; 7) important considerations and strategies to manage cougar-human conflicts; and 8) implementing an adaptive management approach for research that will provide important cougar management information.

CHAPTER 1

THE NEED FOR COUGAR MANAGEMENT GUIDELINES

In October 2002, a group of wildlife managers, biologists, and scientists gathered in Boise, Idaho to discuss the need for management guidelines for cougars (*Puma concolor*). All of the participants agreed that cougar management should include: an adaptive management approach, elements that protect and maintain viable cougar populations, habitat protection for cougars and their prey; consideration of diverse stakeholder values, regulated hunting, and integration with the conservation of other wildlife species.

We called ourselves the Cougar Management Guidelines Working Group (CMGWG). Our group consisted of 13 professionals with more than 200 years of cumulative experience in cougar management, policy, and research. In June, 2003 the tragic death of Ian Ross while studying African lions (*Panthera leo*) reduced our number to 12. The Working Group dedicates these Guidelines to Ian, whose pioneering work on cougar and other large carnivores, as well as his initial contribution to the Guidelines, will not be forgotten. Sharon Negri, founder and executive director of WildFutures, convened the CMGWG and coordinated communication over the course of this project.

Management of cougars is difficult for several reasons: cougars are secretive, they exist at low population densities, they impact wild and domestic prey, they can threaten human safety, and public attitudes about them differ widely. In these guidelines, we advocate management rooted in defensible science, and encourage an adaptive management approach designed to maintain sustainable cougar populations across their range. Although cougars are widely distributed in western North America and are not considered endangered, landscapes and human attitudes are changing rapidly and bringing new management challenges. Ultimately, human values, interacting with the biological characteristics of the species, determine management objectives and the means used to achieve them. We offer this synthesis of cougar natural history and management history, methodologies, and strategies as a tool for wildlife managers. **Points of emphasis throughout the document are placed in bold type to draw the attention of the reader.** We hope wildlife agencies use this tool to develop standards for regional management.

THE IMPORTANCE OF COUGARS

Cougars are presently the only large, obligate carnivore thriving in self-sustaining populations across western North America. The species has existed here along with its major prey—mule deer (*Odocoileus hemionus*), white-tailed deer (*O. virginianus*), elk (*Cervus elaphus*), moose (*Alces alces*), and bighorn sheep (*Ovis canadensis*)—for at least 10,000 years (Logan and Sweanor 2001:11-12, 13-14). Ecologically, cougars strongly influence energy flow in ecosystems, are a potent selective force on prey animals, modulate prey population dynamics, indirectly affect herbivory in plant communities, influence competitive interactions between herbivores, and compete with other carnivores for prey (Logan and Sweanor 2001). Moreover, because self-sustaining cougar populations require expansive, interconnected wild land, conservation strategies designed to benefit cougars also benefit an array of other wildlife (Beier 1993, Logan and Sweanor 2001:366).

A conceptual framework developed by Kellert and Smith (2001) identifies 9 types of human values toward wildlife (Table 1.1). Many of these values are manifest in stakeholders that influence cougar management. An appreciation of

An understanding of the diversity of human values toward cougars can help wildlife managers develop a biologically sound and socially acceptable policy.

Table 1.1. Human values toward cougars are diverse; any given person may hold several values. (Adapted from Kellert and Smith 2001).

Value	Description
Naturalistic	Emphasizes personal experiences people have with cougars. Those experiences engage human curiosity and imagination and invoke feelings of adventure, exploration, discovery, and satisfaction of skill in the process of getting close to cougars to either hunt or observe them.
Scientific	Pertains to direct study and understanding of cougars, which foster intellectual growth about nature that can result in practical advantages to people and promote an attitude of caring for nature.
Aesthetic	Refers to the physical attraction of nature to people. Cougars are often featured in art (e.g., photographs, paintings, and sculptures) and other visual media. Cougars invoke impressions of nature's refinement and beauty. Aesthetic perceptions of nature may have evolved in humans through our connection with animals and habitats that gave us sustenance and safety and caused people to hone survival skills.
Utilitarian	Focuses on the practical and material value. Cougar hunting currently provides direct economic value to outfitters and guides in amounts ranging from $2,000 to $4,000 per hunt. Economic benefits accrue to rural communities and specialists (e.g., taxidermists) that provide hunting-related services. Wild landscapes that support cougar and prey populations provide ecosystem services, such as clean water and air, and outdoor recreation opportunities, including consumptive and non-consumptive uses. Cougars also actively contribute to the integrity of wild ecosystems through interactions with prey species.
Humanistic	Acknowledges the emotional connection of people to nature that fosters affection and concern. This value has been demonstrated in the increasing protection for cougars since the mid-1960s and the formation of organizations devoted to protecting cougars (e.g., Mountain Lion Foundation, Cougar Fund).
Dominionistic	Refers to the human inclination to subdue nature. This includes controlling cougars to make the environment safe for people and domestic animals. Hunting cougars to either kill them or partake of them in a non-consumptive way, like observation or photography, can demonstrate an ability to function in challenging conditions and express strength, vigor, and boldness. This includes hunting for pure enjoyment and its competitive opportunities.
Moralistic	Pertains to the ethical responsibility that people have to conserve cougars and to treat cougars with respect. This has been demonstrated by the trend toward greater protection of cougars and regulations governing the treatment of cougars (Minnis 1998, Teel et al. 2002, Gigliotti et al. 2002).
Negativistic	Emphasizes the fear and aversion toward cougars, and anxiety about the risk of attack—particularly to one's self and family. This may be extended to concern over domestic and game animals that represent a source of direct and indirect sustenance. Those feelings may also promote awe and respect for the animal.
Symbolic	The figurative significance of cougars in modern society expressed in children's books and toys, in marketing and advertising, and as symbolic animals for educational institutions and the professional sports industry.

KEN LOGAN AND LINDA SWEANOR

Cougars require large areas to maintain self-sustaining populations.

the diversity of these values, and how values change over time, can help wildlife managers develop a biologically sound and socially acceptable policy.

Policies resulting from close alliances with a few special interests may encourage stakeholders with divergent values to challenge the professional authority of wildlife management agencies (Kellert and Smith 2001, Riley 1998). During the 1990s, stakeholders used the ballot box to ban or curtail sport hunting of cougars in California, Oregon, and Washington (Minnis 1998, Whittaker and Torres 1998). These actions, along with recent public opinion surveys in Colorado (Zinn and Manfredo 1996), Montana (Riley 1998), South Dakota (Gigliotti et al. 2002), and Utah (Teel et al. 2002), indicate that people in the western U.S. are concerned that cougars are not being properly managed.

A BRIEF HISTORY OF COUGAR MANAGEMENT
IN THE UNITED STATES AND CANADA

Unregulated cougar hunting, and habitat alterations that affected prey numbers, caused the near extinction of the cougar in eastern North America. By 1900 cougars had largely been extirpated east of the Rocky Mountains, with the exception of Florida (Young and Goldman 1946, Nowak 1976). Through the first half of the 20th century, management emphasized preemptive eradication. Bounties were paid as an incentive to remove cougars for protection of wild ungulates and domestic livestock. The payments were significant for the time. In the 1920s, California paid bounties of $30 for a female cougar and $20 for a male. In 1945 bounties increased to $60 for females and $50 for males.

Bounties continued to be paid throughout the western states into the 1960s (Figure 1.1), when cougar management shifted to a brief non-bountied but non-protected status. Coincident with the abolishment of bounties, depredation policies became less preemptive and more reactive, targeting cougars associated

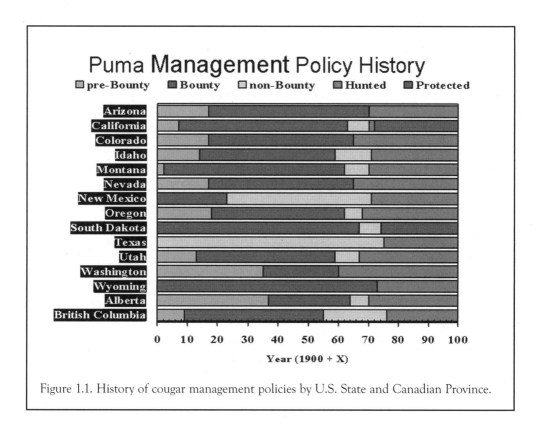

Figure 1.1. History of cougar management policies by U.S. State and Canadian Province.

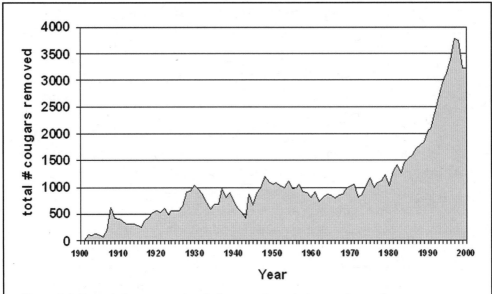

Figure 1.2. Recorded cougar removals (bounty, depredation, and sport harvest combined) from western US, 1902 – 1999. Summaries obtained directly from western states and Canadian province fish and game agencies: AZ, CA, CO, ID, MT, NM, NV, OR, UT, WA, WY; and Nowak (1976).

with livestock losses. By the early 1970s cougars were managed as a game species across most states and provinces (median establishment was 1971). This represented the first form of protection for cougar populations.

Cougar removals are the only consistent and long-term information collected on cougars in western North America. Although these records do not indicate population status, they might provide perspective on past and current impacts on cougar populations. A key assumption is that the records are a reasonably complete record of the number of cougars killed by people.

Many wildlife managers have long assumed that a drop in cougar removals followed elimination of bounties, which then stimulated a widespread cougar population increase. However, Torres et al. (2004) tested this hypothesis and found that cougar removals did not decrease after government-subsidized bounties ceased (Table 1.2). We speculate that cougar numbers, circa 1900, may have been low due to unregulated cougar removal, market hunting of ungulates, competition from domestic livestock, habitat changes during Euro-American settlement, or incidental killing of cougars from poisoning programs targeting wolves (*Canis lupus*) and coyotes (*C. latrans*) (Robinette et al. 1959:271). Therefore, any cougar population increases that may have occurred in the latter part of the 20th century (Proceedings of Fifth Mountain Lion Workshop, State

Status Reports, 1996) cannot be attributed solely to the abolition of bounties. Cougar increases, if they occurred, might more plausibly be attributed to increases in numbers and distributions of deer and elk.

The 1990s exhibited the most dramatic increase in cougar removals (Figure 1.2) since the 1960s (Torres et al. 2004). Increasing human populations during the same period required managers to consider habitat issues, in addition to managing cougar numbers. Wildlife managers cannot assume that these unprecedented removal levels, especially combined with the historically high levels of habitat loss and fragmentation that are occurring, have no affect on cougar numbers.

Although western states and provinces contain large areas of contiguous habitat, urbanization can influence movement of cougars among areas, thus fragmenting (inhibiting movement of animals between habitat patches) cougar habitat and creating barriers to free movement among habitat patches. Therefore these guidelines incorporate strategies to maintain connectivity among populations. Increasingly, these approaches will entail a regional perspective, including management plans that span state, provincial, tribal, and national

Table 1.2. Average annual cougar removals during the last decade of the bounty period (1951-1960) and the first decade of the hunting period (1971-1980). The hunting period also includes depredation removals. Data obtained directly from state and provincial agencies and Nowak (1976).

State	Cougars killed per year (1951-1960)	Cougars killed per year (1971-1980)	Difference
Arizona	238.4	223.9	-14.5
California	153.5	18.2	-135.3
Colorado	60.6	66.1	+5.5
Idaho	73.1	140.5	+67.4
Montana	5.1	73.4	+68.3
New Mexico	12.0	65.8	+53.8
Nevada	106.9	66.9	-40.0
Oregon	109.1	24.2	-84.9
Utah	117.5	171.6	+54.1
Washington	102.1	184.1	+81.9
Wyoming	0	8.8	+ 8.8
Total Average	978.3	1043.1	
Overall Difference			+65.1

boundaries. The future will bring new conservation challenges as habitats are altered and prey and predator populations shift in response. It will also bring changes in the human values listed in Table 1.1. These changes will eventually render these guidelines obsolete. Therefore, we strongly recommend that a standing Guidelines Committee be appointed as a part of the process of conducting periodic Mountain Lion Workshops, to regularly review and update these guidelines.

Our Approach

In these Guidelines, we synthesize current knowledge of cougar natural history, biology, ecology, and management. We present these guidelines as a framework. All aspects of cougar management that we have outlined in these guidelines do not apply to each state or province equally.

We recognize many unknowns and uncertainties about cougars and cougar management, present conflicting viewpoints where they exist, and point out where there is insufficient information. Serious unknowns and uncertainties bedevil attempts to scientifically manage cougars (or any wildlife species). These include uncertainties about basic demographic parameters (population density, growth rate, age-sex structure, survival and reproductive rates), how populations respond to management prescriptions or hunter selectivity, and temporal and spatial variation in these parameters and responses. Despite these problems, management decisions must continue to be made based on the preponderance of evidence from decades of research on wildlife ecology and conservation biology—including an impressive body of literature on the cougar. In light of these issues, cougar management should be structured on these basic principles:

1. A large-landscape approach, on the order of thousands of square kilometers of well-connected habitat with thriving natural prey populations, is necessary for healthy, self-sustaining cougar populations. This is based upon accumulating research results that indicate:
- Cougars are large obligate carnivores that exist at relatively low densities and require large areas to maintain self-sustaining populations (Beier 1996, Logan and Sweanor 2001).
- Dispersal of most male cougar offspring and a large proportion of female offspring, and immigration of male and female cougars, is essential for maintaining cougar populations and for regional gene flow (Beier 1993, Culver et al. 2000, Sweanor et al. 2000, Logan and Sweanor 2001, Ernest et al. 2003, McRae 2004).

2. Given uncertainties about basic demographic parameters, responses of populations to management prescriptions or hunter selectivity, temporal and spatial variation, and understanding that cougar habitat is changing, cougar management should adopt an adaptive management process (below).

3. Cougar management should reflect the full array of human values and input from all stakeholders.

4. In light of the diversity of stakeholders and human values, funding for cougar research, management, and conservation should not be derived solely from hunting-related programs.

ADAPTIVE MANAGEMENT

Adaptive management is characterized by continual monitoring of indicators that measure progress toward achievement of management goals and objectives, changing of management practices when new information indicates that better alternatives are available, monitoring relevant stakeholder values and interests, and the monitoring of natural environmental changes that may affect

Cougar removals are the only consistent and long-term information collected on cougars in western North America. This photograph of successful cougar hunters was taken in 1928.

cougar management results (Meffe and Carroll 1997:358-373, Williams et al. 2002:230). The adaptive management process includes:

1) Clearly stated and justified cougar management goals and objectives.

2) Management actions designed as scientific experiments that allow evaluation of management prescriptions in attaining management goals and objectives. Specifically:
   • Design objectives as questions to be answered or as hypotheses to be tested, along with attendant predictions through experimentation.
   • Monitor effects of management prescriptions in time frames appropriate to the objectives.

3) Assess public stakeholder interests in cougar management.

4) Modification of cougar management based on information gained from management experiments, monitoring, other research, and public stakeholder interests.

Because these guidelines were developed in the spirit of adaptive management, we expect them to evolve over time, too, as better information on cougars and cougar management is made available.

CHAPTER 2

COUGAR-PREY RELATIONSHIPS

Although cougars prey on a wide variety of animals including rabbits (*Sylvilagus* spp), hares (*Lepus* spp), skunks (*Mephitis* spp), porcupines (*Erethizon dorsatum*), beavers (*Castor canadensis*), bobcats (*Lynx rufus*), coyotes, and rodents, ungulates provide most of the prey biomass consumed by cougars throughout their range. In North America it is unlikely that a cougar population can be sustained in the absence of ungulates. The number of prey killed per cougar varies with the number and age of dependent young (Ackerman et al. 1986), season (Ross et al. 1997, Hayes et al. 2000), nutritional condition of the prey (Logan and Sweanor 2001), competition from other predators (Kunkel et al. 1999), and usurpation of kills by scavengers (Harrison 1990). Using an energetics model, Ackerman et al. (1986) estimated that an adult male cougar kills 1 deer every 8 to 11 days, an adult female without kittens every 14 to 17 days, and a female with 3 juveniles every 3.3 days. Connolly (1949) reported that an adult cougar killed 1 deer every 9.7 days during winter. Predation rates on bighorn sheep and mule deer by females with kittens averaged 1 animal every 3-8 days (Harrison 1990). Beier et al. (1995) estimated that each cougar kills about 48 large mammals and 58 small mammals per year.

Shaw (1980) estimated that cougars annually removed 15-20% of the mule deer population on the Kaibab Plateau in Arizona. Anderson et al. (1992) estimated that cougars annually killed 8-12% of the mule deer population on the Uncompahgre Plateau, Colorado. Cougars killed an estimated 2-3% of an elk herd and 3-5% of a deer herd annually in Yellowstone National Park in Idaho, Montana and Wyoming (Murphy 1998). In Alberta, a single cougar killed approximately 9% ($n = 11$) of the early-winter bighorn sheep population including 26% ($n = 6$) of the lambs (Ross et al. 1997).

These percentages, by themselves, do not express the impact on prey populations, because this impact depends on whether predation mortality is additive or compensatory. The impact of predation is greater when mortality due to predation is *additive* to other types of mortality, and less when deaths due to cougars are *compensated* by reductions in other types of mortality, or increases in recruitment.

Adult cougar on an elk kill.

We offer managers the following major principles of cougar-prey relationships (numbers 1, 3, 4, 6, 8, 10 and 11) and our main recommendations for managing these interactions (numbers 2, 5, 7, and 9).

1. If members of an ungulate population are in poor physical condition, cougar predation probably has little net effect on ungulate numbers. When individuals in an ungulate population are in excellent condition, cougar predation can have a large effect on recruitment, and cougar control may increase ungulate numbers.

The ungulate prey of cougars, including deer, elk, bighorn, and moose, have life history characteristics affected by density dependent processes (McCullough 1979, Boyce 1989, Bowyer et al. 1999, Keech et al. 2000). As population density increases and approaches carrying capacity (*K*, the number of animals at or near equilibrium with their food supply—Kie et al. 2003), individuals increasingly compete for resources; fecundity, survivorship and nutritional condition decline (McCullough 1979); and incidence of disease increases (Eve and Kellogg 1977, Sams et al. 1996). These changes lead to low recruitment as *N* approaches *K* (Figures 2.1, 2.2). However, as an ungulate population approaches *K*, weather

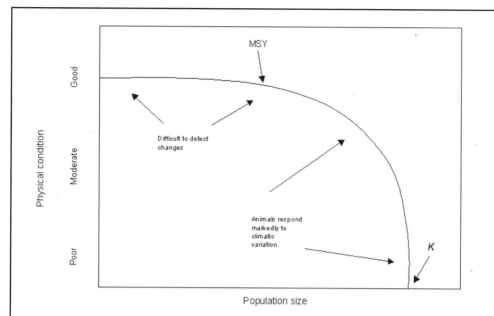

Figure 2.1. Relationship between physical condition of individuals and population density, for a typical ungulate species. There is little change in physical condition (and subsequent changes in reproduction or survival) below the inflection point. As population size approaches carrying capacity, K, physical condition declines markedly, but this can be masked by response to environmental variation (Kie et al. 2003).

and other environmental factors cause increasingly large variability in the population response (Figure 2.2). This can obscure the underlying relationship between population density and recruitment. While ungulate managers seldom know where a population is in relation to K, the body condition of its members may indicate whether the population is below or above carry capacity (Figure 2.1).

Where individuals in an ungulate population are in excellent nutritional condition, predation by cougars will have a larger effect on the rate of increase than if the prey are in poor condition. Any animal removed from a population well below K probably would have survived if not preyed upon, and probably was not hindering reproduction or survival of other individuals through competition. Under these circumstances, cougar predation is largely additive mortality that slows the growth rate of the prey population. However, in a prey population in poor condition, where individuals are restricting the reproduction and survival of conspecifics through competition, cougar predation helps lower prey population density, reduces competition, and increases the likelihood of survival and reproduction for the remaining individuals in the prey population

(Caughley 1979, Bartmann et al. 1992). Under those circumstances, cougar predation is compensated for by increased recruitment and survival of remaining prey (compensatory mortality). Mortality caused by predation in this scenario has little depressing effect on the prey population (Bailey 1984).

Bowyer et al. (2005) provide a conceptual model for managers to use in determining when predation might have a large impact on prey population size such that the prey population would respond to predator removal. This approach (Table 2.1) relates individual condition and reproductive characteristics of ungulates to the likelihood that the population is subject to additive mortality by predation.

If the goal of management is to maintain large ungulate populations (e.g., to support a large sport harvest), this approach suggests that reducing cougars will only help when the ungulate population is below the inflection point of Figure 2.1, and exhibits characteristics indicated in the middle column of Table 2.1. In fact, predation at high prey density can be beneficial, because it helps prevent damage to range quality, thereby increasing stability of the ungulate-vegetation system (Bowyer et al. 1997, Jordan et al. 2000), and helps maintain ungulate

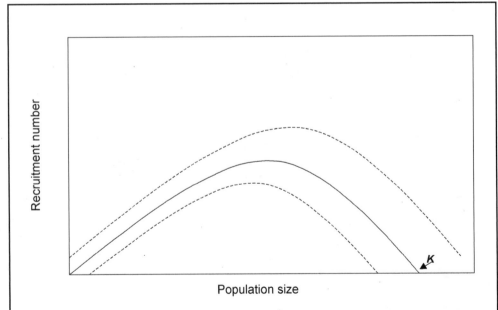

Figure 2.2. Both recruitment of young and variation in recruitment vary with population size of adult females (adapted from McCullough 1979, Bowyer et al. 2000). Variation in recruitment increases as density increases from the peak of parabola to carrying capacity (K) because environmental variation is more able to help or harm ungulates in poor physical condition (adapted from Kie et al. 2003).

body and antler size (French et al. 1956, Anderson 1981, Ullrey 1983, Suttie and Kay 1983).

Low-density traits will be evident in *any* population far below *K*, even if it experiences *no* predation. Therefore, even when the ungulate population is apparently well below *K*, a decision to reduce cougar numbers only makes sense when the manager has data that indicates cougar predation is the strongest limiting factor operating on the ungulate population. Furthermore, if there is no alternate prey (i.e., cougars subsist almost entirely on the ungulate of concern), cougar numbers will (after a time lag) decline even without increased cougar harvest.

2. After a sudden decline in prey carrying capacity, an increased cougar harvest may help avoid problems caused by a time lag in the response of cougars to changes in prey.

Changes in cougar populations in response to prey densities may involve time lags that may be problematic for managers (Logan and Sweanor 2001). For

Table 2.1. Life-history characteristics of ungulates that reflect the relative differences in a population regulated by predators versus food (Bowyer et al. 2005).

Life-history characteristic	Population size mainly affected by predation[b]	Population size mainly affected by food
Physical condition of adult females	better	poorer
Pregnancy rate of adult females	higher	lower
Pause in annual production by adult females	less likely	more likely
Yearlings pregnant[a]	usually	seldom
Corpora lutea counts of adult females[a]	higher	lower
Litter size[a]	higher	lower
Age at first reproduction for females	younger	older
Weight of neonates	heavier	lighter
Mortality of young	additive	compensatory
Age at extensive tooth wear	older	younger
Diet quality	higher	lower

[a] Some species of ungulates may show limited variability in these characteristics.
[b] These traits will be evident in *any* population far below *K*, even if it experiences *no* predation. The manager should have evidence of significant mortality due to predation before concluding that reducing predation would increase ungulate recruitment.

Adult male cougar stealing a kill.

instance, when the number of their primary prey declines, cougars may switch to livestock and pets (Torres et al. 1996), or other species of wildlife (Jorgenson et al. 1997, Logan and Sweanor 2001). In these circumstances, a moderate to high cougar harvest may reduce the rate of decline of the ungulate population, competition among cougars, impacts on livestock and pets, and potential risk to humans. However, it is possible that vacancies created by the loss of resident adult cougars may be filled by immigrating subadults (about 10-30 months of age) in the short-term, resulting in increased densities.

3. We suspect that cougar predation can keep a prey population at an unnaturally low density (a "predator pit").

Holling (1959) demonstrated that additive mortality due to predation could interact with density-dependent prey dynamics (Figure 2.2) to create either 1 or 2 stable equilibrium densities for the prey population. The theoretical basis is strong, and it is plausible that such dynamics exist for some predator-prey systems. In vertebrate predator-prey systems, the higher equilibrium (near but somewhat below the carrying capacity set by food resources) is considered the natural state of affairs, but following a catastrophe (such as severe winter weather, drought, a tornado, a disease epidemic, or isolation of a population segment by a barrier), mortality from predation can, in theory at least, keep prey at an equilibrium far below food-based K—a situation referred to as a "predator pit" (Haber 1977, Bergerud et al. 1983, Messier 1994).

Predator pits have been postulated to occur for caribou (*Rangifer tarandus*) interacting with wolves in Alaska (Ballard et al. 1997), for moose interacting with wolves (Messier 1994), for pronghorn (*Antilocapra americana*) interacting with coyotes (Dunbar et al. 1999), for wild horses (*Equus caballus*) interacting with cougars in Nevada (Turner et al. 1992), and for bighorn sheep interacting with cougars in California (Hayes et al. 2000, Schaefer et al. 2000) and Arizona (Kamler et al. 2002). In addition, cougar predation caused the near extinction of porcupines in a Nevada basin (Sweitzer et al. 1997). We believe that some of these situations probably do represent predator pits. However, we caution that the existence of a 2-equilibrium system has never been demonstrated in nature or in the laboratory. Many, perhaps all, unmanaged ungulate-predator systems could have a single equilibrium prey density (Messier 1994).

Mule deer are a major prey source for cougars in the western United States.

4. The presence of: a) alternative prey; b) excellent prey condition and reproduction; c) high mortality due to predation; and d) historic evidence of a much larger prey population suggest the existence of a predator pit.

A predator pit occurs only in multiple-prey systems (Gasaway et al. 1992) where alternative prey provide a subsidy that keeps cougar numbers high. In a putative bighorn pit, for instance, cougar numbers would rapidly decline (via emigration, or low survival or reproduction) as predation reduced bighorn numbers, unless alternate prey (such as cattle or deer) sustained cougars at densities where they regularly encounter bighorn.

Because predator pits, by definition, are far below K, the prey population of concern should exhibit the characteristics of a population well below K (Table 2.1), namely excellent physical condition and high fecundity. If individuals in the prey population exhibit poor physical condition, then a predator pit does not exist.

Finally, if a predator pit exists, there must be evidence that the prey population had the potential to be several-fold larger than at present. Data on predation mortality are best obtained from radio-tagged prey.

Cougar predation may limit some small, isolated bighorn populations.

These 4 conditions are necessary, but not sufficient, to prove the existence of a pit. Conclusive demonstration would require precise measurements of how cougar numbers and numbers of prey killed per cougar vary with prey density (Messier 1994)—measurements which can probably never be made at any reasonable cost. Nonetheless, a persuasive case exists when these 4 conditions are met.

5. Managers should use an adaptive management approach to design meaningful case studies of potential predator pits involving cougars.

When a manager finds that a predator pit is the most plausible explanation for non-recovery of a prey population, a manager may choose to propose cougar control for a number of years. Opponents will also argue that even if the management action is followed by prey recovery, the recovery may have occurred even without cougar control. The argument, in a nutshell, is that management action to control cougars to benefit one prey population is an unreplicated case study, proving nothing. However, a well-designed scientific study can provide reliable information on cougar-prey relationships. Chapter 6 offers further advice on using management actions as research efforts to reduce scientific uncertainty.

6. Cougar predation may limit some small, isolated bighorn populations.

Cougar predation has been an important factor in the decrease of bighorn sheep populations in California (Hayes et al. 2000, Schaefer et al. 2000) and Arizona (Kamler et al. 2002). Ross et al. (1997) found no relationship between the density of alternative prey and cougar predation on bighorn sheep, suggesting that the high rate of predation on bighorn was a result of encounter rate and not prey switching. Logan and Sweanor (2001) came to a similar conclusion for a bighorn sheep population in southern New Mexico. Wehausen (1996) implicated cougar predation in the decline of bighorn sheep across several subpopulations in the Sierra Nevada. However, habitat abandonment in response to predation risk by cougars—rather than direct predation mortality—was hypothesized to be the cause of low reproduction rates, and resultant population declines, of bighorn sheep in the Sierra Nevada. Cougar predation on bighorn sheep appears to be sporadic (Sawyer and Lindzey 2002). This variability may be caused by individual cougars becoming specialists at preying on bighorn sheep (Ross et al. 1997), by changes in densities of primary prey (Schaefer et al. 2000, Logan and Sweanor 2001), by differences in the probability of cougars encountering bighorn sheep, by time lags in prey switching, or by small differences in habitat characteristics among populations (Kamler et al. 2002).

Skeptics of predator control often argue that cougars and bighorn coexisted for several thousand years in the western United States, and that it is therefore unlikely that cougar predation limits bighorn sheep populations today. However, during the past 150 years, some bighorn sheep populations have been decimated by diseases carried by domestic sheep, some residual populations have become isolated by roads and urbanization, cow-calf operations in the habitats of some populations provide an alternative prey subsidy (thus increasing the likelihood of cougar presence), and fire suppression in the habitats of some populations have decreased forage quality, increased ambush cover, and increased densities of mule deer (thus plausibly attracting cougars).

7. Targeted removal of cougars could benefit small bighorn sheep populations limited mainly by cougar predation.

For populations of bighorn sheep with more than 15 ewes, modeling of cougar predation on bighorn sheep has suggested that indiscriminant predator removal is not more effective in reducing extinction risk than would be selective removal of individuals that specialize in killing bighorn sheep (Ernest et al. 2002). Indiscriminant predator removal creates vacancies that are likely to be filled by dispersing juveniles. Indiscriminate predator control may remove individuals that did not frequently kill bighorn sheep, but will be replaced by individuals that do. Finally, if alternative food sources such as deer were readily available, a constant and extremely high level of cougar removal (i.e., more than 28%) might be necessary to prevent rapid recovery of the cougar population (Logan and Sweanor 2001). This level of predator control may not be acceptable to the interested public. For those reasons, where bighorn sheep populations are threatened, selective cougar removal is recommended.

8. Cougars select vulnerable prey, and are adaptive, opportunistic predators.

Numerous authors have described the gender, age class, and condition of prey killed by cougars. Hornocker (1970), Spalding and Lesowski (1971), Shaw (1977), Ackerman et al. (1984), and Murphy (1998) all suggested that vulnerability of individual prey may be the most important factor in their selection by cougars. Those investigations identified individuals in younger or older age classes, or in poorer condition, as being selected by cougars. Nowak (1999) found selection by cougars for younger deer and elk. Among adult deer and bighorn sheep, cougars also may prey on males selectively (Hornocker 1970, Ackerman 1982, Harrison 1990), especially when males are in a weakened condition following the rut (Robinette et al. 1959, Shaw 1977, Harrison 1990), or during drought (Logan and Sweanor 2001). Ross et al. (1997) reported selection for young bighorn sheep by cougars. Pierce et al. (2000a) reported that

ART LAWRENCE

Sierra Nevada bighorn sheep.

cougars selected deer in young and old age classes, and that females were selected among adult deer. Preference for females among adult mule deer also has been reported for other populations of cougars (Bleich and Taylor 1998). Recent investigations suggested that cougars do not select prey in poor condition (Kunkel et al. 1999, Pierce et al. 2000a); however, bone marrow fat has been the primary index used to determine prey condition by most investigators. Although the percentage of bone marrow fat was not related to prey selection by cougars (Kunkel et al. 1999, Pierce et al. 2000a), they selected for older animals. Thus, percentage of marrow fat may not adequately reflect vulnerability of an animal to predation by a cougar (Pierce et al. 2000a).

Size of prey may affect selection by cougars. Cougars in Montana selected deer over elk, and elk over moose (Kunkel et al. 1999). However, Nowak (1999) found no preference between deer and elk.

Sex and age of a cougar likely affects its diet (Murphy 1998, Anderson and Lindzey 2003). Ross and Jalkotzy (1996) reported that male cougars were more likely to kill moose than were females. Solitary cougars may be more likely to eat smaller prey than will females with kittens (Ackerman 1982). Ackerman suggested that killing large prey to provide for their offspring would be a desirable strategy for mothers, and populations of cougars could not exist in areas devoid of large ungulate prey. Pierce et al. (2000a), however, reported that female cougars with kittens (less than 6 months old) were significantly more likely to kill young deer (less than 1 year of age) than were single female or male adults. Birth pulses of cougar populations often coincide with the birth pulse of their primary prey (Logan and Sweanor 2001, Pierce et al. 2000a), suggesting that timing of reproduction in cougars may be influenced by the availability of vulnerable, young prey.

Variation in prey selection is notable for some populations of cougars as vulnerability or availability of prey changes. During the wet season in coastal California, cougars increased predation rates on feral pigs (*Sus* sp.) (Craig 1986) and, in Utah, they killed twice as many black-tailed jackrabbits (*Lepus californicus*) during winter (Ackerman et al. 1984) when compared to summer. Adult male deer may be taken at a higher rate during winter when they are in a weakened condition from the rut (Robinette et al. 1959, Shaw 1977). The vulnerability of newborn calves results in high depredation rates on cattle in Arizona (Shaw 1977, Cunningham et al. 1995).

9. Determining prey selection requires a comparison of diet with availability of prey.

Litvaitis et al. (1994) distinguish between *use* and *selection* of foods by wildlife. *Use* simply indicates the relative amount of food consumed, and can be based on proportion of prey items or prey biomass comprised of a particular item. *Selection* implies that a food item is exploited disproportionately to its availability in the animal's home range. According to these definitions, an observation by agency personnel that mule deer (or adult male mule deer) comprise 60% of cougar prey carcasses encountered probably says little about *use*, and even less about *selection*. This observation would reflect use if the prey carcasses encountered were an unbiased sample of prey taken by cougars, but would not reflect use if some prey items are easier to detect than others, or if the habitats searched by the personnel are not representative of the landscape. Documenting selection is even more difficult, as it requires measuring availability of prey, which in turn is a function of the abundance and behavior of each prey item.

BECKY PIERCE

Bobcat on its kill. Competition between cougars and other carvinores is an important factor affecting predator-prey dynamics.

10. Cougars affect, and are affected by, other carnivores in their ecological systems.

In the ecological systems that cougars inhabit, both exploitative and interference competition with other predators probably occurs. The diets of wolves (Kunkel et al. 1999), coyotes (Pierce et al. 2000a, Harrison 1990), bears (*Ursus* spp.) (Murphy 1998), bobcats (Koehler and Hornocker 1991), and jaguars (*P. onca*) (Iriarte et al. 1990) overlap extensively with that of cougars. Differential habitat and prey selection may allow for coexistence of cougars with those other carnivores. In some instances, scavenging of their caches by other carnivores causes cougars to increase predation rates (Harrison 1990). Cougars kill smaller carnivores. Koehler and Hornocker (1991) reported cougars did not feed on bobcats they killed, and Beier and Barrett (1993) reported that cougars killed and ate bobcats and coyotes. Conversely, cougars have been killed by packs of wolves (White and Boyd 1989, Boyd and Neale 1992). Those observations suggest that competition is an important factor affecting the predator-prey dynamics of multipredator systems that include cougars.

11. Cougars affect the structure and diversity of ecological communities.

The important prey species of cougars in North America are often sympatric with each other. Limitation of population growth by predation may help to increase species richness by decreasing competition (Paine 1974) or by increasing niche partitioning (Hutchinson 1957, MacArthur 1972) within the prey community (Longland and Price 1991, Pierce et al. 1992). As the availability of one prey species increases, predation by cougars may switch to that prey species, affecting its population growth. This may reduce predation on a competing prey species and allow for both prey species to coexist. Competition from cougars also may increase species richness among smaller predators by disproportionately influencing the numbers of one species more than another (Terborgh et al. 1999). This can happen through direct and indirect competition for prey or through direct predation on smaller predators. For example, cougars compete directly with coyotes for mule deer in the eastern Sierra Nevada. As cougar populations decreased, predation on mule deer by coyotes increased (Pierce et al. 1999a). Coyotes probably compete more directly with foxes and bobcats than with cougars; therefore, the presence of cougars may benefit those other smaller species. Because cougars kill and cache large prey, other carnivores and bird species benefit by scavenging (Hornocker 1970, Pierce et al. 1998, Beier 1995).

CHAPTER 3

COUGAR HABITAT

Cougars have the broadest geographic distribution of any terrestrial mammal, except humans, in the western hemisphere, using elevations from sea level to over 4,500 m (Logan and Sweanor 2001). Although there are no reports of reproducing cougar populations in desert flats, agricultural landscapes, or large grasslands, cougars use almost every other vegetation type, including coniferous and deciduous forests, woodlands, swamps, savannahs, chaparral, gallery riparian forests, desert canyons and mountains, and semi-arid shrub lands (Hansen 1992).

This broad distribution of cougars is a testament to the species' ability to persist in almost any habitat that offers adequate prey and cover. Nonetheless, habitats can vary significantly in quality. In particular, adequate abundance, distribution, and vulnerability of large ungulate prey are necessary to support cougar populations in North America (Ackerman 1982, Pierce et al. 2000b, Logan and Sweanor 2001). The availability of more than one species of ungulate helps maintain cougar populations during declines in the abundance of one major prey species (Logan and Sweanor 2001). Cover is provided by vegetation or rugged terrain. Cougars use cover for stalking prey, security, and raising their young (Seidensticker et al. 1973, Logan and Irwin 1985, Laing and Lindzey 1991, Logan and Sweanor 2001, Laundré and Hernandez 2003).

Quality of cougar habitat is also affected by land use. High densities of humans and roads decrease habitat quality for cougars by increasing the potential for cougars to be killed on roads, depredation incidents involving pets, and policies favoring removal of cougars to reduce the potential for attacks on humans. In addition, cougars may be directly affected by other large carnivores through increased mortality caused by predation. Indirectly, other large carnivores might influence the abundance and distribution of prey species used by cougars (Boyd and Neale 1992, Minta et al. 1999, Kunkel et al. 1999, Ruth 2001).

Despite their ability to use many habitat types, and their ability to disperse over large expanses, cougars live at low densities and thus are vulnerable in isolated habitats and to habitat changes that impede or preclude movement

Cougars are wide-ranging, cryptic mammals that cannot be easily surveyed and monitored.

among habitat patches. Accordingly, we assert that habitat conservation is an essential component of cougar management, and should involve efforts to identify, map and protect cougar habitat and the landscape linkages that join them.

We assume that managers have 3 objectives in identifying and managing habitat for cougars. First, cougars are wide-ranging, solitary mammals that cannot be easily surveyed and monitored. Therefore, **identifying habitat is the best starting point for defining populations** to which all other management prescriptions will be based.

Second, **managers conserve cougar habitat to increase population resiliency.** Managing wildlife species through the management of their habitat is an indirect but effective wildlife conservation tool, already well developed by the 13th century (when Kublai Khan managed large areas for food and cover for game birds [Polo and Latham 1958]). The approach involves identifying habitat characteristics sought or used by a particular species, identifying where these characteristics exist, developing strategies to conserve these characteristics, and applying these strategies where the greatest benefits will accrue. Leopold (1933) considered habitat management more progressive than population management (the direct manipulation of populations by hunting, predator control and captive propagation), and advocated the integration of habitat and population management. In particular, habitat management can buffer against the uncertainties inherent in population management. That is, when populations fall to lower than desired levels, the presence of abundant, quality habitat provides for resiliency that would not be possible if habitat were only marginal in its ability to support the target species.

Third, managers **conserve cougar habitat because it has an umbrella effect for biological diversity**. Large carnivores, because of their size, low population density, and trophic position, require more space than other terrestrial species. Thus, if plans are devised for the long-term management of these low-density species, many other species will benefit from the "umbrella effect" (Soulé 1985, Noss 1991, Soulé et al. 2003). Because populations cannot be conserved without habitat management, managing cougar habitat is central to this approach to conservation.

Most habitat management has been directed toward ungulates and game birds rather than carnivores. These efforts typically involve detailed characterization of the vegetation and landforms used at different times of the day, seasons, and years. For cougars, we recommend a simplified approach based on large-scale assessments of presence-absence, habitat quality assessments based on characteristics known to influence cougar populations, prey distribution, and a landscape approach to integrating subunits into a larger picture. We recommend the following:

1. Map cougar habitat in an accessible, modifiable format.

It is critical that each state or province map cougar habitat. The state and provincial wildlife agencies are probably best suited to do this because they have wildlife professionals on the ground and direct access to wildlife reports and historical recording systems. Universities and non-government organizations could collaborate with the state agency to produce these maps. Such collaboration can be a constructive step in engaging some stakeholders in cougar management.

Historic range maps (e.g., Young and Goldman 1946, Leopold et al.1981, Logan and Sweanor 2000) are rarely detailed enough to provide a useful state-wide map, but some states or provinces may have more specific local maps of cougar distribution at various points in time. In most cases, a map will need to be created from scratch. Locations of cougar presence can be based on harvest records, depredation, road kill, track counts, remote camera documentation, and distribution maps for ungulate prey. We recommend maintaining a database of the data layers that underlie the map. The database should include the type of observation, date, and geographic precision of each location. For instance, harvest records usually are attributed to a management unit, and thus are less precise than some other types of data.

This map has 2 applications: it indicates current distribution and provides a system to monitor changes in the distribution of cougars over time. We recommend a process similar to that used by the California Department of Fish and Game (CDFG) to map cougar habitat for California (Torres and Lupo 2000). First, CDFG used California's deer distribution map to roughly approximate the distribution of cougars. This was augmented with records of cougars, including depredation kills, and exact locations of radio-collared deer and bighorn sheep that were killed by cougars during CDFG research projects. In the next step, the preliminary range map was overlaid on a habitat map to eliminate habitat obviously not suitable for cougars, such as lakes, urban areas, and agricultural development. At this point, the map was considered a reasonable and accurate depiction of cougar habitat in the state of California. CDFG further refined the map, using the California Wildlife Habitat Relationship model, to rank cougar habitat by quality into 5 levels, from "high suitability" (e.g., mixed chaparral) to "little or no suitability" (e.g., saline wetland) to "outside range." Although this final map of California cougar habitat is crude in some aspects, it is an important tool from which agencies and the general public can assess changes in cougar habitat through time, and more importantly, work to enhance and protect the integrity of cougar habitat (Figure 3.1).

2. Identify and map subpopulations as a network of sources and sinks.

For any large area, the cougar habitat map (developed as described earlier) will usually have areas of good habitat that are nearly (or perhaps completely) surrounded by non-habitat or marginal habitat. Where urban areas, freeways, reservoirs, canals, or broad swaths of inappropriate vegetation are likely to impede cougar dispersal movements, these impediments define the edges of habitat patches, each of which corresponds to a cougar subpopulation. By using habitat and landscape features the manager can map potential subpopulations and create a map of the regional cougar metapopulation structure (Chapter 4). We suggest that these subpopulations be named or numbered, and used as geographic units for managing cougar harvest (Chapter 6) and cougar habitat. In some cases, subpopulations may be defined on the basis of management decisions that create areas with markedly different mortality.

Many cougar metapopulations consist of source populations (where mean growth rate is positive) and sink populations (where mean growth rate would be negative in the absence of immigration). We suggest that managers state whether they intend to manage each identified subpopulation as a source or as a sink. For instance, if a subpopulation exists in an area with low prey density and little ambush cover, it could be designated as a sink for management purposes. Alternatively, a sink might be mapped in an area where human values

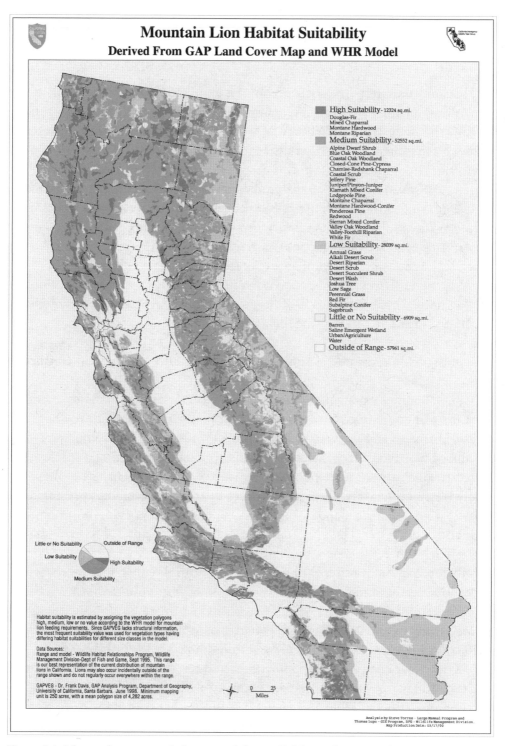

Figure 3.1. Map ranking cougar habitat suitability in California (Torres and Lupo 2000).

and land-use decisions make it likely that road kills, sport-hunting, or depredation removals will outpace reproduction. In either case, the manager would be
aware of the need to maintain immigration to avoid local extirpation.

This guideline treats the designation of a population as source or sink
primarily as a matter of setting a management objective, rather than selecting
the label that reflects a population's growth rate in the absence of immigration.
Although the inherent tendency of the land to support a positive or negative
growth rate should be a factor in this designation, that rate is rarely known.
Furthermore, most subpopulations probably have (or once had) the *potential* for
positive growth, so this guideline acknowledges that negative growth rates
(sinks) are the results of human decisions about cougar management and land
use. Although the use of metapopulation theory is an important biological
principle, it is equally important as a management principle. Metapopulation
theory promotes larger regional management, emphasizes the importance of
"non-traditional" habitats such as linkages, and the recognition that subpopulation status is expected to vary independently (source, sink).

3. Manage areas designated as sources for low mortality and human conflict.

Subpopulations experiencing negative growth rates (sinks) cannot persist
over time without connectivity to adjacent subpopulations (source areas) or
intrusive management actions (augmentations). The concept of **refugia** was
introduced in evolutionary literature to refer to the contraction of a species into
limited residual habitat in response to climatic or ecological change. However,
in conservation literature, the concept refers to areas protected against human
impacts, where ecological and evolutionary processes can operate most naturally
(Noss and Scott 1997). The term **natural refugia** is often applied to managed
areas where human access is restricted, but not precluded, by lack of roads or
trails or topographic features of the landscape. Natural refugia may be scattered
throughout managed areas and have no legal, long-term protected status.

Managing a source population of cougars requires managing an area for low
or no cougar harvest, low road density, minimum potential for livestock conflict, lightly exploited ungulate populations, and few opportunities for human-
cougar conflicts. Source areas that are managed with these objectives in mind
function as refugia or "biological savings accounts" that contribute to cougar
population resilience by producing dispersing subadult cougars to augment,
both numerically and genetically, more heavily exploited sink areas (Logan and
Sweanor 2001). Source areas managed for low levels of cougar harvest are
essential to long-term persistence of cougars in sink areas and, ideally, will
provide an area where natural selection processes may operate within a cougar

population. However, managing a cougar subpopulation as source population is not desirable in areas with high densities of humans or livestock because they may lead to increased human-cougar conflict and decreased public support for cougar management. Establishing management objectives for source and sink areas provide managers with an opportunity to design management strategies to protect cougar habitat and the landscape linkages needed to ensure healthy populations.

National and state parks, where hunting and other land uses are regulated, often provide legally secure areas for cougars and should be considered in mapping refugia for metapopulation analyses. The size of refuge areas needed to ensure cougar population persistence, however, depends on cougar prey densities and other factors affecting vital rates. Beier (1993) and Logan and Sweanor (2001) suggested that a *minimum* reserve size of 1,000-2,200 km^2 is needed to sustain a cougar population for 100 years. Some *de facto* cougar reserves (e.g., national parks) may not meet the recommended reserve size suggested by Beier (1993) and Logan and Sweanor (2001), but they may function as part of a refugia that would reduce the need to legally or administratively establish *additional* protected areas. However, the ability of these areas to function as refugia should be confirmed rather than assumed. Explicitly mapping and managing certain areas for source populations ensures that a decision to reduce cougar numbers in one area is made only in conjunction with the overall management goal for the affected metapopulation.

4. Assess and map the status of, and threats to, each subpopulation.

Maps depicting protection status and threats will affect the designation of a subpopulation as a source or sink, and are essential to managing for connectivity. We recommend GIS layers for:

- Land ownership and level of legal protection. Public land (i.e., land managed by federal and state governments) forms the core of most cougar populations in the Western United States (Logan and Sweanor 2001). Because lands vary in their conservation mandate, maps of protected status should indicate the specific management regime (e.g., multiple-use, designated wilderness, research natural area, or national parks) of mapped parcels. For the same reason, the map should distinguish among private, state, tribal, and federal lands. Land ownership and protection status can usually be constructed as a single GIS layer.
- Paved roads, highways, canals, and railroads, all of which present barriers or filters to cougar movement. Highways, canals, and railroads can be included on a single GIS layer. Road density (kilometers of paved road per km^2) is better displayed as a separate layer.

- Land use: agricultural, industrial (including major mines and oil and gas projects) or urban uses. The land use map would have already been used to generate the cougar habitat map (above).
- Parcel maps. Maps indicating existing and approved subdivisions are probably the single most useful indicator of the likelihood of future conversion to urban or densely roaded land uses. Zoning maps are much less useful in this regard, but can sometimes be an indicator of land prices. Development can isolate cougar habitat into islands (Beier 1993, Torres and Lupo 2000, Ruth 2001, Cramer and Portier 2001).
- Geographic data on cougar harvest densities, road kills and locations of cougars removed for depredation or public safety.
- Seasonal ranges of major prey species.

Maps of livestock grazing allotments might also be useful because they may suggest areas where depredation conflicts and cougar removals may occur. However, there are usually insufficient data to map differences among allotments in stocking levels, husbandry, and operator philosophy—factors that are more meaningful than existence of the allotment. Maps depicting logging and recreational activities may not have long-term utility. However, **managers may wish to map a few heavily-used trails that occur in prime cougar habitat**, such as Sabino Canyon near Tucson, Arizona, where a tram brings more than 2,000 visitors per day 8 km up the main perennial stream in the Santa Catalina Mountains. This type of development and associated human disturbance may result in increased human-cougar interactions. It may also change cougar numbers or distribution by affecting cougar behavior and/or prey distribution; or result in increased removal of *nuisance cougars* (defined in Chapter 7).

5. Identify linkages using GPS collars, surveys for sign, or GIS analyses.

Connectivity is essential to maintaining the metapopulation structure of cougar populations (Chapter 4). Cougars occupying small tracts—or even large isolated tracts—are at high risk of extirpation (Chapter 4). In some areas, cougars and their prey need linkages to accommodate migration between winter and summer ranges (Pierce et al. 1999b). The first steps in assessing or maintaining connectivity are described in previous guidelines in this chapter. The next step is to describe the extent of existing or potential connectivity. Landscape scale genetic analyses (Culver et al. 2000, Sinclair et al. 2001, Anderson et al. 2004, McRae 2004) can identify populations that are or were recently linked. GPS animal-tracking collars programmed to obtain locations at night will provide fine-grained movement paths of collared cougars.

As a stopgap placeholder until a linkage can be more rigorously defined, it is reasonable to map a potential linkage along the shortest or most direct route between subpopulations. In some cases, there will be only one remaining non-urban route which can immediately be mapped as the only potential linkage.

GIS modeling of animal movement or permeability can also be useful (Beier et al. 2005). However, we caution that these models usually extrapolate habitat-use data to predict cougar movement. Even when movement data (e.g., Dickson et al. 2005) are used to perform an analysis of landscape permeability, all GIS analyses involve assumptions, estimates, and extrapolation. Therefore we urge analysts to conduct sensitivity analyses to determine model sensitivity to varying parameters in the model.

Surveys for cougar sign in potential connective habitat offer a promising approach to identifying connective habitats for cougars, but the scarcity of sign in sub-optimal habitats between cougar subpopulations will make it difficult to devise an efficient and inexpensive protocol. Locations of cougars killed along roads passing through a potential linkage may be one source of "free data" but

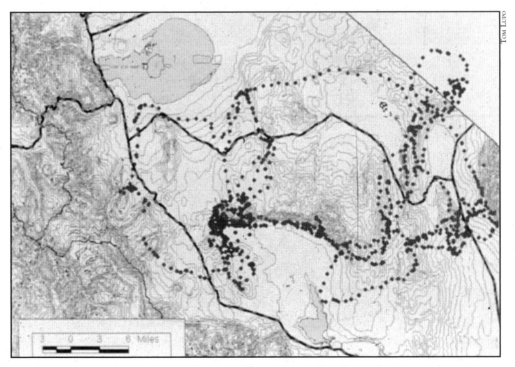

GPS animal-tracking collars programmed to obtain locations at night will provide fine-grained movement paths of collared cougars.

Growing human population can fragment suitable cougar habitat.

STEVE TORRES

identify only one point along a corridor that might extend kilometers from the road to the next cougar subpopulation. Hair snares (barbed carpet pads with olfactory and visual attractants) have been successfully used to detect some felids, including lynx (*Lynx canadensis*) (McDaniel et al. 2000) and ocelot (*Felis pardalis*) (Shinn 2002), suggesting that an array of hair snares in potential cougar corridors could identify specific travel routes and characteristics of preferred travel paths. However, when hair snares that induced rubbing by captive cougars were placed near kill sites of 4 wild cougars, the animals ignored the snares (Beier, unpublished data). Although these results are discouraging, modifications may produce a more effective hair snare. Dogs specifically trained to find cougar scats might provide another promising approach. Track surveys can also be efficient in areas where suitable substrates, such as dirt roads or sandy streambeds, are well distributed in the area of interest. Although conventional radio-tracking is a useful tool to identify connective habitats used by cougars (Beier 1995), Global Positioning System (GPS) technology will provide better data to address connectivity issues. We support development and testing of sign-based approaches to identifying optimal corridors for cougars. We recommend a random (or stratified random) sampling scheme to identify the best connective habitat. We discourage surveys confined to areas that the biologist expects to be optimal, or that are easiest to survey; such designs guarantee that no cougar sign will be found in the types of areas in which no surveys occur.

6. Assess the quality of each linkage.

As described in the introduction to this chapter, quality depends on abundance and diversity of prey, suitable cover, and land uses. The distance between the subpopulations to be connected approximates the length of the linkage. GIS analyses can refine this estimate by additionally considering how cougar movement responds to vegetation, topography, and land use.

Beier and Loe (1992) distinguished between a travel corridor (which offers enough resources for passage in a single movement event lasting no more than a few days) and a live-in corridor (which can support resident individuals and be part of an individual home range). A live-in corridor obviously requires higher habitat quality. For cougars, distances less than 10 km in length probably would be adequately served by a travel corridor and distance more than 50 km in length probably require a corridor of live-in quality. Harrison (1992) suggested that a live-in corridor for cougars should be about 8 km wide. Our understanding of cougar movement does not indicate which type of corridor should be planned for linkages 10-50 km long.

Beier (1993, 1995) studied a highly fragmented and human-impacted environment in southern California and found cougars using narrow corridors crossing urban areas. Beier's study was limited to travel corridors less than 8 km in length. More research is needed to address both travel and live-in corridors, preferably using improved technology such as GPS collars.

7. Conserve and restore linkages.

The decision about whether to invest in conservation or restoration of a linkage hinges on the actual or restorable habitat quality, length and area of the linkage or potential linkage, public acceptance, and the cost to acquire, restore, and manage the linkage. Highways, urbanization, canals, and agricultural development can disrupt cougar dispersal. Beier (1995) found that urban areas

Contrary to popular belief, cougars do not avoid water.

are impenetrable to movement of both adult and juvenile cougars. Similarly, large expanses of agriculture, such as in California's central valley, and major freeways, such as Interstate 15 through the Tehachapi Mountains of California and Interstate 15 between the Santa Ana and Palomar Ranges of California, coincide with significant gradients in gene flow (Ernest et al. 2003). Bobcats and coyotes have experienced marked genetic divergence in response to a 40-year-old freeway in California (S. Riley, R. Sauvajot, National Park Service, unpublished data). Similarly, McRae (2004) found that Interstate 40 coincided with the most pronounced genetic differentiation of cougars in his 4-state study area (Arizona, New Mexico, Utah, Colorado). The role of Interstate 40 is unclear, however, because other freeways in the study area did not seem to present barriers to gene flow. It is possible that topographic features associated with Interstate 40, and not the road alone, contributed to this pattern.

Maintaining or restoring habitat connectivity for cougars (and other species) will require landscape-level analyses and collaboration among wildlife managers, land management agencies, county and regional planners, transportation agencies, private landowners, and others. Perhaps the most comprehensive effort to date is the South Coast Missing Linkages effort, which began in 2001 in southern California (Beier et al. 2005). In 2003-2004, similar efforts began in New Mexico (Mark Watson, New Mexico Game and Fish Department, Santa Fe, personal communication), Arizona (Evelyn Erlandsen and Norris Dodd, Arizona Game and Fish Department, Phoenix, personal communication), and Colorado (Monique DiGiorgio, Southern Rockies Ecosystem Project, Denver, personal communication).

The enthusiasm of all parties for the efforts in Arizona, California, Colorado, and New Mexico demonstrates that planning for habitat connectivity has become a mainstream approach. Nonetheless, landscape linkages are often a pale remnant of natural connectivity, and there are lingering concerns about whether cougars (or other animals) will actually use corridors in a way that promotes demographic and genetic processes (Simberloff et al. 1992). In urban southern California, Beier (1995) found that 5 of 9 dispersing subadult cougars found and used at least one of the 3 corridors in the study area, and that all corridors were used. Although sample sizes (9 dispersers; 3 corridors, all less than 7 km long) were limited, this provides strong evidence for the utility of corridors for cougars.

Simberloff et al. (1992) also raise the issue of potential negative effects of corridors. Although Beier and Noss (1998) found no evidence for any of these ill effects, in part this may reflect a lack of research effort. Of particular relevance to cougars is the risk that highway crossing structures within a corridor, such as underpasses and culverts, could funnel prey into areas where predators would exploit high prey density, creating a prey trap. Little et al. (2002) reviewed the literature and found no empirical support for this idea. Dickson et al. (2005) documented that cougars in southern California do not exploit such structures. However, most crossings on that study area occurred where major roads crossed narrow, degraded habitat corridors, where cougars and their prey may not wish to linger. Cougars may behave differently where such crossing structures occur along roads passing through large blocks of intact habitat. One possible negative effect of corridors used by cougars, is the potential increase in cougar-human interactions.

8. Provide incentives to landowners to protect habitat.

Private lands are especially important to cougar conservation efforts where those lands provide low elevation winter ranges for prey and where they provide linkages between blocks or patches of cougar habitat. Conservation easements, land purchases, and incentives to private landowners to protect critical habitats and linkages for major ungulate prey species are an important consideration in developing cougar conservation plans.

9. Consider augmentation as a last-resort alternative to natural connectivity.

Although current distribution and abundance of cougars in the western US and Canada have not required managers to undertake augmentation or reintroduction, these alternatives may become important in the future. Management of the Florida panther (*P. c. coryi*) illustrates the importance of these activities for a cougar population. Translocation of Texas cougars to increase genetic diversity of Florida panthers apparently succeeded in reducing the incidence of several medical conditions and improving survival rates (Land et al. 1999, Shindle et al. 2001). In addition, establishing a population of panthers outside of south Florida (a requirement for de-listing) probably will require reintroduction, because restoring natural connectivity through central Florida may be impossible.

Although augmentation and reintroduction can be useful tools, and are central to recovery of the Florida panther, we urge managers to use such strategies only as a last resort. Certainly, managers should never approve a project that severs natural connectivity under the rationale that cougars can be periodically translocated to maintain demographic and genetic processes. First, translocation is expensive and often unsuccessful. In Arizona, 2 translocated cougars did not stay at the release site, but moved 30-80 km where they started attacking livestock (Shaw, personal communication). Translocated cougars in California similarly did not stay in their release areas and experienced high mortality (Christensen and Fischer 1976, p 150). Ruth et al. (1998) translocated 14 cougars over 320 km in New Mexico. Eight of these animals died within 4 months, 4 animals (including 3 subadults) did not return to the release area, and 2 males returned to the area where they were originally captured.

More importantly, translocation and reintroduction require planning, careful implementation, and long-term monitoring. The total costs probably exceed the cost of maintaining a semblance of natural connectivity. Finally, a semi-natural cougar linkage benefits other species that also gain demographic and genetic benefits from the same linkage. Because translocation and reintroduction do not serve this "umbrella" function, they should be considered only as a last resort.

Chapter 4

Assessing Cougar Populations

Seidensticker et al. (1973) hypothesized that cougar populations are governed by a land tenure system that limits adult density to prevent harm to food supply and guarantee sufficient resources for breeding members. Logan and Sweanor (2001) tested and rejected this hypothesis. Their data were consistent with a "2 reproductive strategies" hypothesis that cougar social systems evolved to maximize individual reproductive success. They found cougar predation could slow prey population growth or contribute to a decline in prey populations. Similarly, Pierce et al. (2000b) demonstrated cougars do not space themselves to sequester prey and do not exhibit a land tenure system, and they concluded that cougar populations are limited by prey availability, not by social behavior. Logan and Sweanor (2001:336-337) also concluded that cougar populations are ultimately limited by prey abundance and vulnerability.

For most wildlife species, age at first reproduction is generally calculated only for females because most population models simulate only females, and because population growth rate is sensitive to the onset of reproduction for females (but not for males). Although litters have been born to females as young as 17-19 months of age (Maehr et al. 1989, Logan and Sweanor 2001), the mean age of females at first parturition is about 24-30 months for captive cougars (Anderson 1983) and 27-29 months of age for wild cougars (Ashman et al. 1983, Logan and Sweanor 2001).

Robinette et al. (1961), Hornocker (1970), and Anderson (1983) suggest that an interbirth interval of 24 months is typical when litters survive to disperse, but that some successful mothers can reproduce at intervals of 12-15 months, and a cougar that loses her litter rapidly comes into estrus and breeds again. Average interbirth intervals have been reported as about 17 months (Logan and Sweanor 2001) to about 24 months (Maehr et al. 1991, Lindzey et al. 1994).

Observations of 327 litters across many studies suggests a mean litter size of about 2.7, with litters of 2 or 3 about equally common (38% each), followed by litters of 4 (14%) and 1 (9%) (Anderson 1983). For 53 litters observed less than 49 days postpartum, Logan and Sweanor (2001) observed a mean of 3.0 kittens per litter; about 50% of the litters had 3 kittens and litters of 2 or 4 kittens each comprised about 25% of the total. Gestation is about 92 days (Anderson 1983, Beier et al. 1995, Logan and Sweanor 2001).

Young become independent at 10-18 months of age, but may continue to associate with their mother or siblings for several weeks. Dispersal occurs at 10-18 months (Anderson et al. 1992, Maehr et al. 2002, Sweanor et al. 2000). Regardless of population density, almost all male offspring disperse (Sweanor et al. 2000), typically moving 85-100 km and occasionally more than 200 km (Anderson et al. 1992, Sweanor et al. 2000). Typically 50-80% of female off-spring remain in their natal population; the philopatric female either replaces a female resident or establishes a home range that partially or fully overlaps with other breeding females (Sweanor et al. 2000). Estimates of survival rate of dependent young range from less than 50% to more than 90% (Hemker et al. 1982, Anderson et al. 1992, Beier and Barrett 1993, Logan and Sweanor 2001), and probably varies with age (Logan and Sweanor 2001:118-119). Adult survival estimates vary from 52-100% and probably are relatively constant with age (Lindzey et al. 1988, Anderson et al. 1992, Beier and Barrett 1993, Logan and Sweanor 2001).

Sex and age composition of cougar populations vary with changes in survival, reproduction and recruitment. Among resident adults, females typically outnumber males. Resident adults comprise 47-82% of non-hunted populations (Seidensticker et al. 1973, Hemker et al. 1984, Logan and Sweanor 2001) and 32-50% of a moderately hunted population (Logan 1983). Subadults (about 10-30 months of age) include non-breeding independent offspring before and after dispersal, female offspring remaining in the population, and male immigrants that may or may not eventually establish residency. They comprise 0-50% of populations (Seidensticker et al. 1973, Hemker et al. 1984, Logan 1983). In isolated populations, subadults may include frustrated dispersers who apparently do not breed (Beier 1995, Maehr et al. 2002). Dependent young range from 0 - 60% of the population (Seidensticker et al. 1973, Hemker et al. 1984, Logan and Sweanor 2001).

Estimates of density of adult cougars vary from a high of 3.6 per 100 km^2 in the Diablo Range of California (Hopkins et al. 1986) to a low of 0.21 - 0.42 per 100 km^2 in Big Bend National Park, Texas (Krausman and Ables 1981).

Cougar populations are capable of rapid growth when recovering from reduction. Peak annual growth rates of 24% were observed following removal of 36% of yearling and older cougars (Lindzey et al. 1992, and peak annual growth rates of 28% were observed following removal of 58% of yearling and older

The cougar kittens, pictured above, are estimated to be between 5 and 6 months of age. Dependent young range from 0 to 60% of the population.

cougars (Logan and Sweanor 2001). During 10 years of no exploitation, a New Mexico cougar population that had been exposed to heavy control efforts before the study period exhibited density-dependent growth that declined from 17% to 5% per annum (Logan and Sweanor 2001:170). Maximum growth rate reached 21% in an Alberta population (Ross and Jalkotzy 1992) and a Wyoming population doubled in size over 3 years after 2 years of intensive harvest (43%) followed by 3 years of 18% harvest (Anderson and Lindzey in press).

Causes of death include intra-specific killing, hunting, injuries sustained during prey capture, vehicle accidents, and starvation (Lindzey et al. 1988, Beier and Barrett 1993, Ross et al. 1995, Logan and Sweanor 2001). In a non-hunted cougar population, killing of young by adult males is a leading cause of death among subadults (Logan and Sweanor 2001). Adult males also occasionally kill other adult males and adult resident females; a female killing other females is suggested (Lindzey 1987), and may rarely occur. Human-caused mortality is the main cause of death in cougar populations that are sport hunted or heavily controlled because of livestock depredations (Hornocker 1970, Murphy 1983, Smith et al. 1986, Logan et al. 1986, Ross and Jalkotzy 1992, Cunningham et al. 1995).

Causes of cougar mortality include intra-specific killing, hunting, injuries sustained during prey capture, vehicle accidents, and starvation.

In all species, population growth is determined by births, deaths, immigration, and emigration. In cougar populations, immigration and emigration patterns differ by sex, with almost all males but a minority of females attempting to disperse out of their natal population. Thus cougar populations depend on immigration for recruitment of virtually all breeding males and about a third of breeding females (Sweanor et al. 2000). Overall, Sweanor et al. (2000) found that immigration provided more recruits than locally born progeny. Inter-population dispersal is therefore a critical process in cougar demography.

We recommend that managers consider the following principles and guidelines in evaluating cougar population status and in managing cougar populations:

1. Recognize metapopulation and source-sink structure.

Immigration and emigration occur during *dispersal*, or movement, of a cougar from its natal area to an area where it attempts to breed. Dispersal is the main process that links one subpopulation (group of potentially interbreeding cougars in a semi-isolated habitat patch) to another. A collection of semi-isolated subpopulations linked by dispersal events (including recolonization events) is termed a *metapopulation*.

Few cougar populations are completely isolated. Analyses of microsatellite DNA suggest cougars recolonized most of North America during the last 10,000 years, and that only one subspecies of cougars occurs north of the Mexican border (Culver et al. 2000). Genetic similarity over large areas indicates high gene flow among putative populations, presumably driven by the obligate nature of male dispersal (Sinclair et al. 2001, Anderson and Lindzey in press, McRae 2004). Loxterman (2001), Walker et al. (2000), Ernest et al. (2003), and McRae (2004) found that desert expanses coincide with significant genetic structuring in western cougars. Thus unsuitable habitat impedes (but does not preclude) dispersal movements. These data on genetic structure and gene flow are consistent with high rates of dispersal across unsuitable habitats, including desert flats and some human-altered habitats (Sweanor et al. 2000). In light of these studies of inter-patch dispersal and genetic patterns, each western state should consider cougars to be distributed as a metapopulation in which subpopulations are (or ought to be) linked by regular dispersal events.

Game management units are typically delineated by rivers, edges of mountain ranges or major vegetation zones, political boundaries, major roads, or ungulate populations. Despite the convenience of these approaches, we believe that the low density and metapopulation structure of cougar populations justifies cougar management units that are appropriate to the species. The first step would be mapping cougar distribution in the state on the basis of survey or harvest data, or the distribution of prey, vegetation, land use, and topographic landforms (Chapter 3). By interpreting this map, and considering potential source and sink subpopulations and likely dispersal routes, managers can delineate meaningful cougar management units.

2. Consider metapopulation and source-sink structure in managing cougar harvests and populations.

When cougar management is based on units with non-biological boundaries, managers need to appreciate that management units (even those based on reliable cougar distribution data) will rarely contain independent populations. Failure to recognize metapopulation structure can lead to management errors. For instance, a particular mountain range managed as a hunting unit may be able to sustain harvests of 30% (e.g., a minimum of 11 cougars were harvested in each of 7 consecutive years in Nevada's Ruby Mountain Range, which had an estimated 35 animals—Ashman et al. 1983, page 19). If managers ignore the likely role of immigration in sustaining the population, they would *incorrectly* conclude that all adjacent hunting units could be sustainably harvested at this level. In a cougar population depleted by over-harvest or natural causes, immigration of males and females from nearby unexploited populations is an important, and sometimes critical, factor in population stability or recovery (Stoner 2004).

Logan and Sweanor (2001:385-390) proposed a zone management framework that recognizes that cougar metapopulations typically exist as a mosaic of sources and sinks. In states where exploitation or removals for depredation may create or intensify population sinks, it is important to manage adjacent cougar populations in a manner that provides immigrants at the rate desired. Zone management is explored in more detail in Chapter 6, and *refuges* (areas managed as permanent source populations) are discussed in Chapter 3.

Dispersal is a critical process in maintaining cougar populations and sustaining natural patterns of genetic diversity. Therefore, landscape fragmentation that disrupts cougar dispersal can seriously impact cougar population dynamics, metapopulation structure and persistence (Beier 1993, 1996, Roelke et al. 1993, Sweanor et al. 2000, Logan and Sweanor 2001). Chapter 3 provides guidelines relating to conservation of habitat linkages.

3. Complete enumeration by sex and age class is expensive and lacks estimates of precision, but is the only way to estimate numbers of migrants and reproducing adults.

All or most cougar researchers believe that the most reliable estimates of density (cougar numbers per unit area) are derived from long-term radio-telemetry studies that attempt to mark all animals in the population. This approach requires the researcher to radio-tag most of the population, monitor sign to detect untagged individuals, use track characteristics to assign untagged animals to sex and age class, and confirm many of these assignments by subsequent capture. Although these estimates have no formal mathematical basis other than simple counting, and lack statistical confidence intervals, we endorse them as the "gold standard" against which indices or other estimates should be compared (Seidensticker et al. 1973, Hemker et al. 1984, Logan and Sweanor 2001). However, we acknowledge that some attempts are more rigorous than others, and that even the most diligent researcher probably fails to detect some transients and an occasional resident cougar.

Most importantly, unlike any of the methods described below, the detailed field study can sort "adult" numbers into segments for subadult transients, breeders, sterile adults, immigrants, and emigrants. Non-breeding transients or sterile adult residents cannot be identified by methods relying on camera traps, distance estimators, tracks, or other means. Thus whenever these other meth-

The most reliable estimates of cougar population density are derived from long-term radio-telemetry studies.

ods are used, the manager must bear in mind that the estimated number of "adults" will include some full-sized animals that are not breeding animals. If the manager wants information on immigration or emigration rates, there is no substitute for a detailed, long-term radio-tracking study with intensive marking efforts.

Although complete enumeration provides the most reliable estimate of population size, this does not mean that managers should attempt complete enumeration. The more important issue is whether a manager needs an estimate of population size at all. Caughley (1977:12) cautions that, "Estimates of abundance have no intrinsic value and should never be considered ends in themselves. The majority of ecological problems can be tackled with the help of indices of density, absolute estimates of density being unnecessary luxuries." Of course, scientists and managers agree that reliable data are always "nice to have," but limited resources and clear management need are over-riding factors in allocating resources to collect data.

4. Capture-recapture estimators are potentially reliable but have not been used on cougars.

Capture-recapture estimators are reliable when assumptions are met, and have the advantage of yielding measures of precision (variance), which can be used to construct confidence intervals. In general, the assumptions of these estimators (Williams et al. 2002) can be met in a well-designed cougar study. However, the method rarely yields accurate and precise methods for populations under 50 (because at lower N, each change of one animal marked or recaptured can have a large impact on the estimate). Furthermore the calculation requires a large number of marked animals (often over 50% of the population) and a large fraction of these must be recaptured (Caughley 1977). Probably because of these problems, and the related high cost of having a large study area in which many cougars are captured and recaptured, conventional capture-recapture studies may be impractical for cougars. Only Anderson and Lindzey (in press) have formally (complete with estimate of variance) used these estimators to estimate population size, although they are often used informally in intensive capture and radio-tracking studies as evidence that few untagged animals exist in the study area.

In the near future, however, 2 new types of capture-recapture estimators may become available—namely using camera stations or "genetic fingerprinting" of cougar DNA in hair or fecal samples. The camera-based method has been used to estimate tiger (*Panthera tigris*) (Karanth and Nichols 1998) and ocelot (*Felis pardalis*) numbers (Trolle and Kery 2003). Genetic fingerprinting of hair has been used to estimate grizzly bear (*Ursus arctos*) numbers (Mowat and Strobeck 2000), and Ernest et al. (2002) demonstrated that cougar feces can be used for genetic fingerprinting. Either method could be implemented over a large area (satisfying the need for many individuals), and both approaches are non-invasive. Either method would probably be much less expensive than a conventional mark-recapture estimate. Camera-based estimators would require being able to reliably identify each photographed cougar, a task that may be abetted by advances in computerized pattern-matching software. Another issue with these 2 methods is accurately estimating the effective area sampled to derive density estimates (Trolle and Kery 2003).

5. Distance-sampling estimators are reliable, but they require helicopter surveys within 2 days of snowfall.

Like mark-recapture estimators, these methods also yield measures of precision. However, they do not yield estimates by sex or age class. Of the many types of distance-sampling estimators in existence, one variant, *line-intercept probability sampling*, has been used to estimate cougar density from track surveys conducted from low-flying helicopters over a study area with fresh snow. Using this procedure, Van Sickle and Lindzey (1991) estimated 14.2 +/- 6.3 cougars in a south Utah study area where 14 cougars (9 adults, and 5 kittens over 1 year of age) were known to be present. The method assumes 100% detection of track sets that cross the transect line. Van Sickle and Lindzey (1991) detected tracks of each of the 4 radio-collared cougars known to have crossed transect lines during the sampling period, and were able to distinguish tracks made before and after the most recent snowfall.

Anderson (2003) evaluated the power of this sampling approach by repeatedly computer sampling empirical track sets generated by cougars equipped with global positioning system (GPS) collars. He determined that helicopter transects spaced about 2 km apart in a 1,710 km^2 study area 2 nights after snowfall had a 90% probability of detecting a 15-18% change in a high to medium density population (2.3-3.5 independent cougars/100 km^2). However, these expectations were not verified by an independent field study.

Safety risks and the requirement to fly within 2 days of snowfall may make this method impractical for routine management purposes. In addition, these density estimates are sensitive to lengths of track sets, which can be difficult and expensive to measure from a helicopter. To circumvent this problem, Becker (1991) and Anderson (2003) propose alternatives to measuring the length of each set of tracks. The survey effort needed to detect a 15-18% change would require about 14 hours of helicopter time if all tracks were not followed from beginning to end and as much as twice that time if tracks were followed. Accuracy and precision improve as distance between transects decreases, and when surveys occur 2 days (instead of 1 day) after snowfall. Future analyses and fieldwork are needed to determine whether estimates are robust to variation in canopy cover or topography.

6. Density estimates should be extrapolated cautiously to larger areas, and more cautiously to other regions.

Cougar populations vary in response to habitat features, prey abundance, and current and past exploitation (Seidensticker et al. 1973, Pierce et al. 2000b, Logan and Sweanor 2001). Cougar density estimates derived from radio-telemetry studies are often used for relative comparisons to other areas or times. However, we caution against extrapolating density estimates from small, local areas to larger areas, such as states or ecological regions, for 2 reasons. First, because cougar researchers tend to go where cougars are abundant, these estimates are probably higher than typical of the larger region. A related issue is

Reports of cougar sightings are the least reliable way to index cougar populations.

that estimates of cougar population density are strongly (r^2 = 0.78) inversely related to the size of the study area (Smallwood 1997). This almost certainly reflects the fact that a small study area will be located in the best habitat, but as study area increases, it includes ever-greater amounts of suboptimal habitat. Thus an excellent density estimate for a small study area probably overestimates cougar density in the surrounding region.

Second, extrapolation is even riskier when an estimate is applied to a region that differs from the study area in: a) vegetation; b) land use; c) topography; or d) management history. Managers should not extrapolate a density estimate unless these 4 factors match well between the study site and the area of interest. Even when factors do match well, the extrapolated density estimate should be continually evaluated in an adaptive approach, and sampling designs should be developed to address problems of extrapolation.

7. Population indices can detect large changes at low cost.

An index is a number that is *monotonically* related to population size, N. "Monotonically" means that the rank-order of an index is highly correlated with the rank-order of population size. The best indices are *linearly* related to N, meaning that a change of 25% in the index reflects a 25% change in N. Indices based on sign are generally assumed linearly related to N, whereas harvest number and catch per unit effort are usually not linearly related to N (Caughley 1977).

Indices can be useful even if they detect only large changes in N. For example, density of Florida panthers was estimated only once (Maehr et al. 1991) and then only in a portion of its range for a single year. Nonetheless, indices such as minimum number known alive, animals encountered per 10 days of capture effort, and expansion and contraction of occupied range were sufficient to persuade most reasonable observers that the population was stable or slowly fluctuating below 70 from 1980-1995, and had grown rapidly since 1995. In a major scientific review on the Florida panther, Beier et al. (2003) concluded that research dollars would be better spent on activities other than estimating panther numbers.

Cougar population trends are commonly (but sometimes not reliably) indexed by monitoring changes over time in cougar sightings, depredation events, harvest level, track counts, and catch per unit effort (often expressed as days of hunting effort per cougar harvested). All of these indices are far cheaper than true population estimates, and often do not require specialized equipment or highly trained personnel. However, indices generally can detect only large changes (25% or more) in population size. Furthermore, some indices are completely unreliable, and others are untested. Indices can best be tested by comparing index results to estimates for a population monitored during long-term intensive capture and radio-telemetry studies, especially if the study population varied widely over the period of study. However, each study provides only one point (with one additional non-independent point for each year of study after the first) in the plot of index versus population size. It will take many studies to fully understand the precision and bias of any estimator. For this reason, untested indices will continue to be used, and it is wise to carefully select only those indices that are most likely to be reliable.

8. Cougar sightings, depredation events, and harvest levels are not reliable ways to index cougar populations.

These 3 methods are not adequate for indexing N or assessing population trend. Reports of cougar sightings are the least reliable because they vary in response to a number of factors, including media coverage of incidents involving cougars. Beier and Barrett (1993) describe 3 cases in which groups of 2-5 experienced witnesses with prolonged, repeated, daylight views of housecats and

Good tracking medium is necessary for using track surveys to assess population trends.

coyotes misidentified these animals as cougars. Although completely unreliable as a population index, clusters of sightings can indicate areas where managers should evaluate the potential for cougar-human encounters (Chapter 7, Holm 2003). Similarly, the number of *depredation events* can change in response to changes in populations of wild prey, shifts toward hobby ranching, changes in numbers and species of pets and livestock, changes in husbandry practices, number of landowners, trends in recreational use, and other factors. Only a careful analysis that controls for changes in these factors can support inferences about changes in cougar numbers based on changes in numbers of depredation incidents. However, these data can help managers identify areas with high potential for human conflict (Chapter 7).

The cougar harvest level probably reflects hunter effort, or cougar vulnerability, more than it reflects cougar numbers. For instance, Aune (1991) found that the number of licenses sold in Montana over a 20-year period explained 82% of variation in cougar harvests. The unreliability of harvest level as a population index is illustrated by the fact that the same data are subject to diametrically opposed interpretations. For instance, anti-hunting factions invariably interpret a marked increase in harvest level over several years as evidence of over-exploitation and imminent risk of population decline. Advocates for predator control or increased hunting invariably interpret the same data as indicating a population increase. Neither inference is reliable.

9. Track surveys, catch per unit effort, or the age-sex composition of the harvest may detect large changes in cougar populations.

Track surveys typically consist of walking in washes, or walking or slowly driving on dirt roads or snow covered routes looking for cougar track sets. Costs are modest; Smallwood and Fitzhugh (1995) conducted a statewide survey for less than $15,000. The simplest methods score each segment of the transect for presence or absence of tracks (Beier and Cunningham 1996). These surveys support construction of confidence intervals, but the level of effort necessary to detect changes smaller than about 25% could be prohibitively expensive (Beier and Cunningham 1996). Another track survey method (Smallwood and Fitzhugh 1995) used the number of individual cougars detected on each transect or transect segment, based on track characteristics, to estimate population trend. However, we do not yet know how sensitive the result is to accuracy in determining numbers of individuals, nor to the problem of non-independence of track sets (e.g., mother and kittens traveling together). One caution worth noting here is that the area of interest must be properly sampled. Road track surveys in the west where roads are not common and often follow drainages cover only a part of an area and a single vegetation type. Potential problems are compounded if most hunting is done from these roads—the index may measure changes in the number of cougars with ranges overlapping these roads and not the overall population. Also, cougar distribution may change seasonally as they respond to migratory movements of prey (Pierce et al. 1999b).

Managers have routinely used measures, such as changes in the number of days of hunting per cougar harvested, as an index of change in population size. As a type of *Catch Per Unit Effort* (CPUE) index, this has a stronger conceptual link to population size than do sightings or depredation incidents. The relationship, unfortunately, is affected by year-to-year changes in snowfall, road access, number of hunters, and quality of guides, and there are no data to confirm or refute the utility of CPUE indices. Furthermore, the difficulty of reliably estimating hunter effort, and small sample sizes, makes using CPUE indices, based on harvest records, questionable (Caughley 1977:17). Researchers have used a CPUE index to estimate numbers of Florida panthers, namely the number of animals encountered during the first 10 days of the capture season, in a situation where effort could be closely controlled (McBride 2001). Because the capture team, season, and procedures were relatively constant for over 20 years, this effort was relatively free of confounding factors.

Anderson and Lindzey (in press) suggest that *age-sex composition of the harvest* may be a useful index of population status. The approach stems from Barnhurst's (1986) hypothesis, based on frequency of road crossings, that subadult males are most vulnerable to harvest, followed by resident males, subadult females, resident females without young, females with older (more than 6 months) kittens, and females with young (less than 6 months) kittens. To test this hypothesis, Anderson and Lindzey (in press) documented the relationship between harvest composition and population trend in a cougar population intentionally reduced by sport hunting and then allowed to recover. Proportion of adult females in the harvest increased, proportion of subadults in the harvest decreased, and age of harvested adult females decreased as the population declined. Similarly, mean age of females in a Utah population decreased as level of exploitation increased, until almost all females in the population and in the harvest were less than 3 years old (Stoner 2004).

We caution that age-sex composition of the harvest is a promising, but unproven, index of population trend, and that it is best interpreted in light of several years of reliable harvest history, and in conjunction with other indices. In particular, this method should not be used to interpret only 1 or 2 years of harvest data. For instance, a harvest comprised mostly of subadult or young adult cougars could indicate a lightly harvested population in which only the most vulnerable animals are harvested. Alternatively, it could indicate that the population had been heavily harvested and the population is comprised mostly of immigrants. Anderson (2003) suggests that monitoring harvests over 3+ consecutive years may allow a manager to distinguish between these 2 interpretations. Shaw (1983) and Laundré and Hernandez (2003) offer guidance on estimating age of cougars.

10. Other indices should be used with caution.

McBride (2002) used minimum number known alive (MNKA) to index the population size of the Florida panther. Although McBride's results are persuasive, the Florida population is isolated, small, and has been subject to 25 years of continuous research. We doubt that MNKA has broad utility for non-isolated cougar populations studied for short periods of time. Beier and Cunningham (1996) speculated that track surveys along the margin of occupied range could detect range expansion or contraction, which would plausibly correspond to increases or decreases in population, respectively. Similarly, McBride (2001, 2002) argued that Florida panther sign in new areas was evidence of a population increase. However, until this method is subjected to more rigorous testing and analysis, we argue that it should not be relied upon for inferences about population trend.

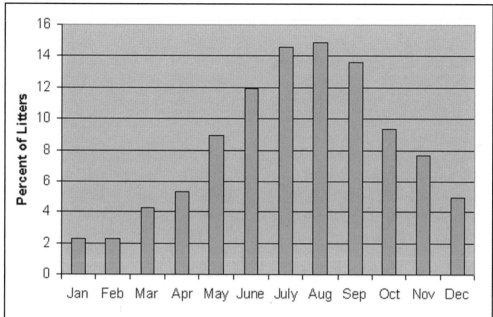

Figure 4.1. Distribution of cougar litter production by month for 302 litters in Colorado (Anderson et al. 1992), Idaho and Utah (Lopez-Gonzalez 1999), Montana (DeSimone et al. 2002), New Mexico (Logan and Sweanor 2001), Nevada (Ashman et al. 1983), Wyoming (Logan 1983), and Alberta (Ross and Jalkotzy 1992).

11. Estimate vital rates only to meet clear objectives.

Caughley's admonition about estimating population size (above) also applies here: estimates of vital rates are not ends in themselves, and managers should seek them only when they serve a particular management purpose. Rates of reproduction, survival, immigration, and emigration are of interest as indicators of population status, and sometimes as parameter estimates in population models (Guidelines 18-21 in this chapter).

Analysis of wildlife populations depends on *proportions* of animals that live or die per unit of time. Raw numbers of deaths or births are relatively meaningless. For cougars, survival rates can only be estimated from radio-telemetry data and product-moment estimators that accommodate staggered entry and censored observations (Williams et al. 2002). There are few *age-specific* estimates of survival rates for cougars. Instead, survival is usually estimated for 3 *stages*: kitten (0-year olds, or until independence); subadult (independent pre-breeding cougars up to 2 or 3 years); and adult (breeders). Because these stage classes probably correspond to marked changes in risk of mortality, and because it would be prohibitively expensive to obtain age-specific estimates, we endorse the use of stage-specific rates.

Reproductive rates include age at first reproduction (usually estimated only for females), litter size, interbirth interval, and percentage of females breeding. In the next subsections, we describe the reliability of estimates of each vital rate, and caution against pitfalls in interpreting data.

12. Survival rates can be estimated only by following the fates of individuals over time.

Survival rates should be calculated only on the basis of exposure days of individual cougars followed over time, accounting for the date at the start of monitoring, and right-censoring any cougars that the researcher loses track of. These simple procedures are clearly described by Pollock et al. (1989) and treated in greater detail by Williams et al. (2002:343).

We caution managers against 2 intuitively appealing, but unreliable methods of estimating survival rate. One unreliable method is to compare numbers of individuals in different age classes. For instance, Maehr and Caddick (1995) divided mean number of Florida panther kittens in litters observed at 12 months of age by the mean size of other litters observed shortly after birth. The result provides an estimate of survival rate only under the unrealistic and unverifiable assumption that reproduction and survival rates do not vary among years; small temporal fluctuations cause large errors in the estimate. Furthermore, this approach disregards the loss of complete litters. Finally, such observations are usually based on animals observed over a range of ages, rather than the 12-month interval required for estimating an annual rate. Another unreliable method is based on the age distribution of animals at death. For example, Shindle et al. (2001: Figure 5) displayed a histogram showing the numbers of panthers that died in each yearly age class. The ratio of adjacent bars in the histogram would reflect survival rates only if the population growth rate and age distribution do not vary over time (Williams et al. 2002:337-342). Because such graphs tempt readers to naïve and probably incorrect estimates of survival rates, we discourage their use.

13. Use caution when estimating or interpreting age-specific or stage-specific rates.

Radio-tagged animals provide the most reliable data for estimating survival rates. However, researchers often are reluctant to radio-tag small kittens. In this case, observing changes in individual litter sizes over time (Logan and Sweanor 2001:117-119, Shindle et al. 2001: Appendix 1) is a valid alternative. However, at 10-16 months of age cubs spend increasing time away from their mothers and, for some litters, it may be impossible to observe the cubs or their tracks during this time. The resulting survival rate estimate will be biased high if the analysis assumes that the missing litters lived and dispersed, biased low if it assumes that the missing litters died, and biased to an unknown direction and magnitude if missing litters are censored. We recommend that such analyses report 3 estimates, corresponding to these 3 scenarios, so that managers can appreciate the uncertainty in the estimate.

Subadult survival rate is the most difficult to measure, in part because all male subadults and about a third of female subadults can be expected to disperse from the study area (Sweanor et al. 2000). Frequent aerial monitoring, including flights far outside natal areas, are essential for obtaining unbiased estimates of this rate.

Calculating adult survival rate does not suffer from these hurdles and pitfalls. However, managers should be cautious when applying survival data from a non-hunted or lightly hunted population to one that is hunted. Although some compensation may occur between hunting deaths and mortality due to intraspecific killing and starvation, it seems unlikely that hunting losses are compensated by reductions in rates of road-kill or injuries sustained during prey capture. Finally, we recommend that survival rates be calculated separately for males and females.

14. Be aware that published estimates of reproductive rates may apply broadly.

Reproductive traits are under relatively strong selection pressure and tend to be species-specific traits with less intraspecific variation than survival rates (Charnov 2001). The mean values for age at first parturition, inter-birth interval, and litter size reported for cougars (Overview section of this Chapter) showed less variation than cougar survival rates and density estimates. Thus, we believe these reported values characterize the long-term averages and frequency distributions for most cougar populations in temperate zones. In the short-term, however, populations probably deviate from these long-term averages in a density-dependent fashion; this issue is defined in Guideline 18 of this chapter, and discussed in subsequent guidelines.

15. Convey information on cougar reproductive biology and survival to cougar hunters so that they can make informed choices about whether or not to kill females.

Although cougars give birth year around, about 73% of cougar births in the western US and Canada occur between May and October (Fig. 4.1). Consequently, during a cougar hunting season that might extend from December through March, more than 80% of kittens born during the previous 12 months are 0-6 months old at some point during the hunting season, and could be orphaned at this age if their mothers were killed by hunters.

Twenty-seven orphaned kittens 0-6 months old studied in California (Beier and Barrett 1993), Montana (R. DeSimone personal communication), New Mexico (Logan and Sweanor 2001), Utah (Lindzey et al. 1989), and Wyoming (K. Murphy and T. Ruth, personal communication) had a survival rate of 0.04, the main cause of death being starvation. In contrast, survival rates of non-orphaned kittens from birth to independence in unhunted populations have been reported to be 0.66 in New Mexico (Logan and Sweanor 2001:117) and 0.67 in Utah (Hemker et al. 1982).

Approximately 40-50% of adult female cougars produce kittens each year, and about 55-85% of adult females are raising dependent kittens each year (Logan 1983, Logan and Sweanor 2001, Ruth et al. 2003). Unfortunately, cougar hunters usually cannot determine if a cougar is a mother before deciding whether to shoot an individual. Distended mammary glands are not always a good indicator of nursing mothers (Logan and Sweanor 2001:375). In addition, Wyoming researchers found that cougar mothers were away from their kittens 50% of the time that the researchers caught family members with dogs in winter (Logan 1983). Moreover, researchers studying cougars in Utah found that kitten tracks were found with their mothers only 25% of the time. They concluded that 75% of mothers would not be recognized by hunters (Barnhurst and Lindzey 1989).

16. Do not assume that all adult females are breeding.

Most studies assume that females of adult size occupying a stable home range are breeding adults, but few studies report apparent rates of female infertility. Beier and Barrett (1993) monitored 12 adult females for more than 12 months with sufficient intensity to detect successful cub rearing if it per-sisted more than 2 weeks. To their surprise, 4 of these 12 females (monitored for 18, 18, 34, and 45 months) never had cubs at heel and did not give birth (or gave birth to litters that did not survive 2 weeks), although each apparently consorted with males (with copulatory vocalizations heard in some cases). The only other study to explicitly address this issue (Logan and Sweanor 2001) monitored 53 adult females. Excluding 7 females that were translocated and 3 that died near expected age of first parturition, 4 of 43 (9%) adult females were not known to produce young. Although these two examples may not be typical they emphasize the need for managers to not assume all adult females are breeding.

17. Rates of immigration and emigration have only been estimated once, but are crucial to understanding metapopulation structure.

Emigration and immigration rates can be measured only in studies that attempt to mark and intensively monitor an entire population (rather than a study area within a large contiguous population). Sweanor et al. (2000) provide the best estimates of emigration and immigration rates for cougars. We suspect their general findings (emigration of most male offspring, emigration of some, but less than half, of female offspring, and immigration supplying a large majority of male recruitment) apply broadly to other cougar populations surrounded by desert habitats. However, the rates doubtless vary somewhat among populations in these ecosystems, and may be quite different in other settings. Although not documented, it is plausible that emigration rates of female offspring are density dependent. Genetic structure across the landscape (Murphy 1998, Anderson et al. 2004, McRae 2004) is related to effective immigration rate (i.e., immigrants that breed), but such analyses do not yield a direct measure of immigration rate (number of immigrants per year, or percent of cohort emigrating or immigrating).

18. Build a population model only when you need to answer a "What if...?" question.

A population model is a mathematical abstraction used to evaluate the conditions (what-if scenarios) likely to produce growth, stability, decline, or extinction of a population or group of populations (Starfield and Bleloch 1986). Game managers frequently use models to estimate how a game population would respond to alternative harvest regulations over the short term. Beier (1993) used a model to assess the impact of losing corridors on persistence of a cougar population in southern California. Models used to evaluate extinction risk are called Population Viability Analysis (PVA) models (Beissinger and Westphal 1998, Ludwig 1999). Ludwig (1999), however, questioned the utility of PVA because it requires too many assumptions, confidence intervals are so wide as to be meaningless, and the underlying data often have large errors. Starfield and Bleloch (1986) provide a common sense overview of modeling for wildlife management. A model can be either *deterministic* or *stochastic* depending on whether it ignores or reflects random fluctuations in vital rates, respectively. These fluctuations include both demographic stochasticity (for example, if the true kitten survival rate is 0.60, the probabilities that a cohort of 2 kittens will have 0, 1, or 2 survivors are 16%, 48%, and 36%, respectively, and the "true mean" of 1.2 survivors is impossible) and environmental stochasticity (unpredictable year-to-year changes in vital rates due to weather, prey, or disease). A model can be *density-dependent* (one or more vital rate changes with cougar density) or *density-independent* (vital rates do not vary with density).

19. Simple spreadsheet models suffice for evaluating short-term harvest scenarios.

In many cases, a manager or biologist may wish to compare population trajectory for a few years under several alternative sets of harvest regulations. If the population is large (say more than 50 breeding females), it is appropriate to use a deterministic and density-independent model, ignoring sources of variation that are important for longer time scales or smaller populations. In these cases, we recommend that managers construct a model in a spreadsheet. With basic spreadsheet skills (knowing how to use formulas, and both absolute and relative cell addresses), a biologist can build such a model in less than an hour. The main advantage of a spreadsheet model is transparency. Because the user builds the model, the biologist or manager can understand exactly what the model is doing, and can tailor the model to run using available data. Results of such modeling efforts can serve as a basis for predicting outcomes in an adaptive management approach as well as determining remedial actions that can be subsequently taken to meet specific objectives.

When managers need to model small populations, or large populations for more than 10 years, it becomes important to consider stochastic fluctuations and density dependence. A mathematically adept biologist can build density-dependence into a spreadsheet model in an hour or two.

Although it is easy to add demographic and environmental stochasticity to a spreadsheet model, stochastic models are usually constructed in a programming language rather than a spreadsheet. The reason is that with a stochastic formula, a single set of input conditions can produce a different result each time the model is run. Because the result of a single run may not be typical, a stochastic model must be run more than 100 times (usually much more) under each scenario to produce a frequency distribution of outcomes (e.g., a frequency distribution of population sizes in year 20, or the fraction of simulated populations extinct at various time durations). Running these hundreds of simulations, compiling them into frequency distributions, and storing the frequency distribution for each scenario is slow and cumbersome in a spreadsheet, but fast and easy in a programming language.

20. Field estimates of annual variation are not appropriate for input in stochastic models.

Algorithms for modeling demographic and environmental stochasticity are straightforward and solidly grounded in probability theory. Demographic stochasticity is modeled solely from probability rules, and does not depend on the user to supply an estimate from field data. However, the model user must specify a value for environmental stochasticity (year-to-year variance in vital rates). Although it seems reasonable to simply use the variance in rates observed in the field, this is not appropriate. The problem is that the observed variance includes both demographic and environmental stochasticity, and using this raw observed value in the model would "double count" demographic stochasticity. Beier (1996) and Gould and Nichols (1998) describe how to partition observed variance into these 2 components, and found that environmental stochasticity was approximately zero for the 3 datasets examined, including 1 dataset on cougars. Failure to make this adjustment would result in overly pessimistic model projections (White et al. 2002).

21. Avoid "canned" population models.

Faced with a need for a density-dependent, stochastic model, managers may be tempted to use a "canned" population modeling package. We strongly urge managers to avoid canned models because they are opaque (the user cannot "see" what is happening) and the required input parameters may not coincide with the data the manager has at hand. Furthermore, most canned packages use unrealistic algorithms for modeling density-dependence, and do not allow the user to tailor the model to fit cougar life history.

If the management issue can be addressed with a simple spreadsheet model, then this type of model should be used. If the management issue demands a stochastic model, then it is too important to entrust to a black box (canned model) and merits the modest investment needed to construct a tailored model.

22. Density-dependent models are required for long-term projections, but we lack the data needed to build them.

Density-independent population models produce increasingly nonsensical results when run for periods of 20 years or more, with simulated cougar populations either reaching absurdly high densities or becoming extinct (Beier 1993). Even worse, population viability estimates for cougars based on density-independent models are unrealistically gloomy (Beier 1993). If even one survival or reproductive rate varies with density, model behavior tends to become stable and projections more reasonable. Thus density-dependent models should be used for long-term projections of cougar populations.

Unfortunately, however, research has not established which vital rates of cougars are density-dependent, much less what equation describes the relationship between a vital rate and cougar density. This is a serious dilemma. Managers must use a density-dependent model for long-term projections, but biologists have yet to produce the data needed to build a density-dependent model. Where does this leave managers?

One option is to give up on long-term modeling. We insist that this is a reasonable option if managers are successfully maintaining connectivity, stopping habitat loss, and limiting anthropogenic mortality (road-kill, hunting, depredation control). In this scenario, the results of long-term predictions of what-if scenarios (What if we lose connectivity? What if road kill increases?) would not cause managers to do anything differently. Resources would best be spent continuing with successful management activities than building a sophisticated model to confirm that a connected landscape is better for cougars than a fragmented one.

On the other hand, sometimes managers need scientific projections to help them decide among management actions, or estimate how much habitat loss or fragmentation can be tolerated. For these cases, we provide a summary of how density-dependence operates in most large mammal populations, and we urge managers to use this information to construct reasonable density-dependent models for cougars, examine the sources of model uncertainty, and cautiously interpret model results.

Eberhardt (1977) hypothesized that for large mammals in general, subadult mortality is most sensitive to density, followed by age of first reproduction, and then reproductive rates. Eberhardt hypothesized that adult survival rate is least sensitive to density, decreasing only when populations reach maximum sustainable levels. Empirical studies of several large mammals generally confirm Eberhardt's model, although few studies measured all of these vital rates, and fewer yet quantified the degree to which density-dependence in each vital rate controlled population growth rate. Our unbiased but incomplete search for literature on density dependence in large mammal populations showed frequent reports of density-dependence in juvenile survival rates (Skogland 1990, Clutton-Brock et al. 1997, Singer et al. 1997, Mduma et al. 1999, Mahoney and Schaefer 2002, Wachter et al. 2002) and age at first reproduction (McCullough 1979, Rachlow and Berger 1998, Swihart et al. 1998, Mduma et al. 1999, Forchhammer et al. 2001, Bonenfant et al. 2002). Based both on the number of studies and the reported strengths of density-dependence relationships, it seems that juvenile survival rate and age at first parturition are approximately equally important in creating density-dependence in large mammal populations. In contrast, our review produced few reports of density-dependent birth rates (Clutton-Brock et al. 1997, Albon et al. 2000, Mahoney and Schaefer 2002) or adult female survival rates (Albon et al. 2000).

Theory and evidence from other species thus suggest that juvenile survival rates and age at first reproduction are most likely to drive density-dependent behavior of cougar populations. But how exactly do these rates vary with population size? Is the relationship linear, curvilinear, or a step function? Fowler (1981) suggests that curvilinear functions are appropriate for most large mammals, with vital rates unchanged from very small to moderately large population sizes, then changing markedly close to carrying capacity (e.g., Figure 2.1). Such a functional form is a reasonable first approximation for modeling. Unfortunately, there are an infinite number of curvilinear equations with steep slopes near carrying capacity (e.g., Beier 1993: Figure 1).

One way to address this uncertainty is to build alternative models, each with a different curvilinear density-dependent function with maximum slope near carrying capacity, as Beier (1993) did for several functions for survival of subadult and juvenile cougars. Beier found that all equations (except the density-independent equation) produced similar long-term projections. Thus, Beier (1993, 1996) developed a reasonable model robust to some sources of uncertainty. Although Beier did not model density dependence in age at first parturition, we believe that this approach can yield useful approximations of long-term cougar dynamics.

23. Managers should not use model predictions without accompanying sensitivity analysis.

Beier (1993, 1996) used his population model to examine how much model predictions (specifically, extinction risk and population size at 100 years) varied with assumptions about density-dependent functions (above), carrying capacity, and other factors. This allowed him to conclude that a habitat area of 1,000-2,200 km^2 is needed to support a cougar population for 100 years, and that smaller patches could support cougars if they were linked by a corridor allowing 1-3 immigrants per decade. This range of sizes (1,000-2,200 km^2) reflects the entire range of reasonable estimates for parameters and functions, and therefore is useful to a manager. It is even more useful because Beier provided graphs showing how model predictions varied with each input factor. A point estimate of minimum habitat area (say, 1,500 km^2) would not have been useful, because it would provide no information on how uncertainties in model parameters affect the estimated minimum area.

By highlighting the parameters that have the greatest influence on model predictions, sensitivity analysis: 1) suggests factors most in need of management attention (e.g., if predictions are sensitive to connectivity but not harvest level, the implications are obvious); 2) identifies parameters that ought to be measured accurately; and 3) gives a general idea of model utility and reliability (e.g., if the predicted minimum area changes by 20% for each 2% change in juvenile survival rate, the model is worthless because we cannot measure juvenile survival that precisely).

Sensitivity analysis is easy to conduct for a spreadsheet model forecasting for 5 years. For a 100-year, density-dependent, stochastic model, several person-weeks of skilled labor will be needed to conduct the analyses and produce clear tables, graphs, and text. But model predictions without sensitivity analysis are at best unworthy of a manager's funding or attention, and at worst dishonest. We urge managers not to rely on any model results that do not include graphs or tables showing how the predictions differ with uncertainty in vital rates, density-dependent functions, and other modeled factors.

CHAPTER 5

DEPREDATION

DEPREDATION POLICIES

After the elimination of bounties 30 to 40 years ago, state agencies established policies to allow the removal of cougars associated with causing property damage or "depredation." Although these policies vary between states (or Canadian provinces), they are all generally similar with respect to:

- Verifying that the damage/loss of livestock can be attributed to a cougar;
- Providing the property owner with information to help protect livestock from future incidents;
- Issuing a cougar kill permit that has conditions specific to the area and time for which the permit is valid;
- Allowing for an agent (typically USDA Wildlife Services) to help property owners remove cougars; and
- Reporting back to the agencies involved with the permit.

In the western United States, depredation incidents have increased over the last 30 years (State Status Reports, Proceedings of the Fifth Mountain Lion Workshop, San Diego 1996). Figure 5.1, which summarizes almost 3,000 depredation permits issued from California between 1972 and 1999, depicts a trend similar to that of many other western states and provinces. Speculation is pervasive about potential causative factors such as declining deer numbers, elimination of bounties, increasing cougar numbers, and changes in land use. Torres et al. (1996) found that depredation problems in California varied regionally for different reasons. For example, domestic sheep depredations were highest in areas adjacent to highly suitable cougar habitat, while pet depredations were most frequent adjacent to newly urbanized areas. In California, approximately 40% of depredation permits result in the killing of a cougar.

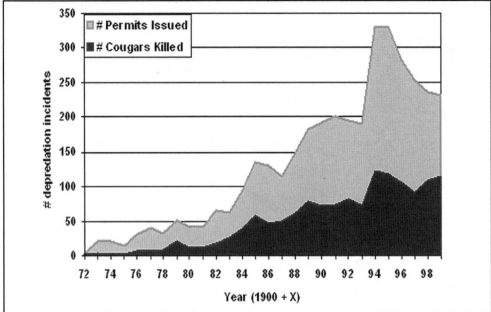

Figure 5.1 Recorded cougar depredation incidents in California from 1972 through 1999. Summaries obtained from the California Department of Fish and Game. (Note: cougar hunting was abolished in February 1972).

We offer 3 broad generalizations about cougar depredation:

Most depredation permits are issued in response to cougars killing domestic sheep.

Depredation records from across the western United States show that cougars have killed domestic sheep, goats, cattle, horses (immature), llamas, alpacas, pigs, dogs, cats, geese, chickens, and emus. Most depredation permits in California (Figure 5.2) and the western United States are issued in response to kills of domestic sheep and goats. Depredation incidents are most common in areas where livestock range adjacent to, or within, cougar habitat. However, with increasing human development in cougar habitats, cougar depredations are becoming more commonly associated with attacks on pets and hobby animals (Torres et al. 1996).

Cougars kill domestic sheep primarily during the summer. Sheep are usually pastured away from cougar country in winter, although cougars occasionally invade fenced pastures on winter range. A cougar may make multiple kills when attacking sheep. Killing 5 to 10 sheep at a site is common; at times many more than this will be killed. Generally only 1 or 2 will be eaten. The cougar may return for several nights and often will kill additional sheep. Most of the dead

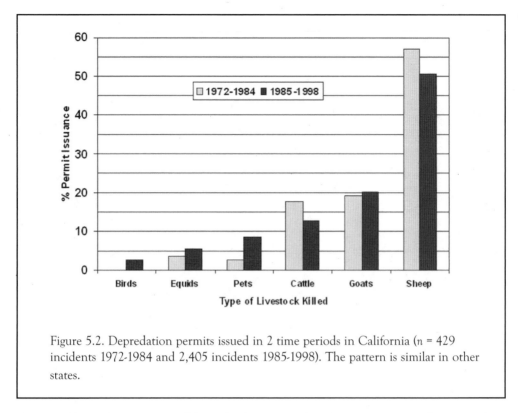

Figure 5.2. Depredation permits issued in 2 time periods in California (*n* = 429 incidents 1972-1984 and 2,405 incidents 1985-1998). The pattern is similar in other states.

sheep will not be covered, although the particular sheep eaten may be carried or dragged for some distance and then covered (Roy and Dorrance 1976).

Cougar depredation on cattle is related to types of cattle management and to the relative abundance of other prey species. Cougars will kill mature cows, but kills of animals over about 300 pounds are infrequent. Cougars mainly kill calves and yearlings. Losses are greatest where calves are born in cougar habitat (Shaw 1977, Cunningham et al. 1995).

Cougar depredation on pets is becoming more common.

In California, cougar depredations on pets and birds (chickens, ducks, and geese) are increasing (Figure 5.2), despite the fact that it is difficult to determine the cause of the disappearance of small animals. This pattern may occur in other western states as livestock operations are replaced by small ranchettes. Torres et al. (1996) determined that pet depredations occur where numbers of new housing starts are relatively high. Unlike livestock, pets are kept close to human residences. These areas are coincident with areas where cougar habitat is being lost, and education on protecting pets and livestock should be focused. Cougar mortality attributed to vehicles and depredation permits also appears to be highest in these areas (Beier and Barrett 1993, K. Logan, unpublished data,

Cuyamaca project) and could represent sink subpopulations. The issuance of depredation permits in these areas should be modified to emphasize preventative education and include a requirement that property owners demonstrate a modification to husbandry practices for repeated incidents.

We offer the following principles and guidelines to help managers evaluate and manage the risk of cougar attacks on pets and livestock:

1. Guidelines for handling depredations should, and typically do, include 6 elements.

During the elimination of bounties 30 to 40 years ago, state and provincial agencies established policies to allow the removal of cougars that caused property damage (depredation). These policies typically include the following 6 elements. We recommend that these 6 elements be included in any depredation policy, and offer guidelines specific to several of them.

- Provide a clear description of the property involved in a damage complaint;
- Inspect attack sites to verify that the damage or loss of livestock can be attributed to a cougar;
- Provide the property owner with information to help protect livestock from future incidents;
- Issue a permit to the property owner to kill one or more cougars within a specific area and time period;
- Allow an agent (typically USDA Wildlife Services) to help the property owner remove the cougar(s);
- Require the property owner to report on cougars removed under the permit.

2. Kills should be inspected within 48 hours to determine if a cougar was responsible.

Cougars are efficient predators and animals killed by them usually show few bite wounds and leave relatively clean cut edges where they feed (Roy and Dorrance 1976). Skinning the neck of medium or large sized prey will usually reveal bite damage, often in the tracheal region and the back of the neck. Numerous bite wounds, on the other hand, usually suggest predation by a canid (Wade and Bowns 1982), although a young and inefficient cougar may inflict multiple bites.

The cougar drags the carcass to a cache site (0-80 m from the kill site), usually covers it with grass, sticks, or other debris when not feeding on it, and typically returns to a deer-sized carcass for about 3 nights, including the night of the kill (Beier et al. 1995). Cougars typically eviscerate their prey and feed on the heart, lungs, and liver first (Roy and Dorrance 1976, Wade and Bowns 1982, Shaw 1983). The rumen is typically not eaten, and is often covered and left a few meters from the rest of the carcass. The carcass is often left uncovered after the last feeding. The presence of cougar tracks in an attack sequence, drag marks, and debris covering the carcass all suggest a cougar killed the animal. Bears or wolves may displace the cougar from its kill, and coyotes, foxes, and skunks often feed on cougar kills (usually after cougar has abandoned the kill, but sometimes earlier). Visitation by these scavengers makes it difficult to attribute the kill to a cougar. In addition, cougars are opportunistic scavengers (Logan and Sweanor 2001, Bauer et al. 2004).

Because of temporal variation in cougar behavior, scavenger visitation, and disappearance of evidence, determination of cougar involvement is probably highly accurate within 24 hours, and reasonably accurate within 3 days of the kill. We therefore recommend that investigations occur within 48 hours. Investigating personnel should be familiar with diagnostic signs of cougar kills (above), and should know how to identify cougar tracks (Shaw 1983).

3. Short-term, non-selective cougar population reduction has not been demonstrated to reduce depredation.

Cougar depredations are an ongoing issue for wildlife managers. Killing a depredating cougar may be only a short-term solution to depredation problems in cougar habitat. Long-term solutions, those that reduce the probability of problems in future, may require significant, ongoing reductions in the cougar population or changes in husbandry practices. On the Spider Ranch in Arizona, essentially all mature cougars on the area were killing calves (Shaw, 1977). Under such circumstances, ranchers may seek a reduction in cougar numbers, rather than the killing of offending cougars. Such reduction programs may be difficult to sustain. In Utah, a cougar population recovered from a 42% reduction in adults in only 9 months (Lindzey et al. 1992). In the more isolated San Andres Mountains of New Mexico, about 31 months were required for a cougar population to recover from a 53 percent reduction of adults (Logan and Sweanor 2001). Actual cougar control programs rarely attain these levels of removal.

Depredation incidents are most common in areas where livestock range adjacent to, or within, cougar habitat.

Research is needed to determine whether cougar control reduces depredation, and whether efforts to reduce the cougar population are more or less efficient than removal of offending animals. A Before-After-Control-Impact design (Chapter 8), in which data are collected on all control and treatment sites both before and after treatment, is more appropriate for studies of the efficacy of predator control.

4. Depredation response should include education efforts to prevent or reduce future losses.

Killing a depredating cougar is only a short-term solution to loss of pets or livestock. Livestock owners can reduce the risk of losing their animals to cougars by changing husbandry procedures. Agencies responsible for wildlife management and for agriculture should make this information available to livestock owners. Agencies can use educational materials developed by agricultural extension offices, other state agencies, or non-governmental organizations (NGOs). The Mountain Lion Foundation, for instance, has initiated community educational efforts to provide information and hold workshops on constructing predator proof fencing in California. The investigating officer should provide the material to the stockowner directly, and may also refer the person to an extension office. Information could include general description on cougar-proof fencing.

Rural residents should avoid feeding deer or other prey species, which may attract cougars that might opportunistically attack domestic animals or even humans. Where cougars may be problems in urban areas, information should be provided regarding the presence of cougars, and how residents can protect their pets and hobby animals (i.e., Wildlife Services: Helping Producers Manage Predation, Department of Agriculture, Animal and Plant Health Inspection Service, Program Aid No. 1722).

Some techniques have not proven effective for reducing cougar predation on free-ranging cattle, and should not be recommended in educational materials without appropriate qualifiers. For instance, the use of guard dogs requires husbandry techniques that restrain herds in limited areas, which may prevent losses of pastured sheep to coyotes (Andelt 1999), but is unlikely to protect calves from the stealthy approach of cougars.

5. Agencies should maintain a database relating depredation incidents to husbandry practices.

Collecting and maintaining a database of depredation incidents is essential to understanding patterns and potential solutions to depredation. For each incident, the agency issuing the depredation permit should record the precise location, date, type of livestock attacked (by age and sex category), husbandry practices, number and type of livestock owned, type of information provided to the livestock owner, and sex, age, and weight of any cougar taken on the depredation permit.

The description of husbandry practices will be most useful for identifying potential solutions. We recommend a narrative describing all husbandry practices on the property, the number and types of animals subject to each practice, and quantitative details about specific methods (e.g., fence height, width of brush-free zones around a paddock, and types of lighting). These details are more useful than checkboxes indicating husbandry practices.

6. Research is needed to determine the effectiveness of husbandry in reducing depredation.

Agencies should analyze their data on husbandry practices (above), publish the results of these analyses, and use the findings in educational materials. Most depredation reports describe husbandry practices that failed to protect the domestic animals. Thus the strongest findings from these analyses will be suggestions of what does not work. Even this information is useful, however.

Dog killed by cougar. To prevent or reduce future depredation losses, rural residents should be educated about the potential impacts of feeding deer or other prey species.

Furthermore, some landowners will report multiple husbandry practices (e.g., pens of 2 different sizes or designs, changes in husbandry practices over time) that will suggest the relative value of different strategies.

The efficacy of husbandry practices in reducing livestock losses has not been adequately evaluated and can only be evaluated in a regional assessment on working ranches. Replication and comparison groups are critical to making rigorous conclusions about efficacy. If wildlife agencies lack the resources or expertise for such a study, they may partner with agricultural agencies or university researchers in agriculture programs. A detailed synthesis of the history of cougar depredation management throughout the range of the species is badly needed, along with ongoing evaluation of existing programs. Such evaluations can occur only where a high level of trust exists between ranchers and the investigators.

Experiments could investigate the efficacy of several reasonable strategies, such as (a) shortening the livestock birthing season, (b) adjusting the birthing season to the period of highest abundance and vulnerability of wild prey, or (c) corralling combined with harassment or hunting of cougars in surrounding habitats (Mazzoli 2003).

CHAPTER 6

SPORT HUNTING

In most state and provincial cougar management programs, sport hunting of cougars provides recreation and serves as a tool to address concerns about cougar predation on wild and domestic animals and potential threats to humans. In justifying sport hunting, agencies tend to emphasize only hunting's utility as a tool to benefit other species. As a result, there is decreasing public support for the idea that sport hunting for recreation is a legitimate use of this resource. As interest groups increasingly challenge hunting programs (Laundré and Clark 2003), it is becoming apparent that many agencies lack data and analyses to design or defend hunting programs.

Although most cougars are harvested with the use of trained hounds, others are taken incidentally during other game seasons, by spot and stalk, or predator calling. In Arizona, between 1982 and 1987, approximately 60 percent of all cougars killed were taken with the aid of hounds (Arizona Game and Fish Department 1987). Hunters who were pursuing deer, elk, or other game species, or who were hunting cougars using other means, killed the remaining 40 percent. During 1991-1997, 93% of cougars killed in Wyoming were taken with hounds (Wyoming Game and Fish 1997, Mountain Lion Management Plan).

When used as a tool, sport hunting usually aims to reduce cougar populations. Although only one study (Anderson 2003) demonstrated that sport hunting reduced a cougar population, it is unlikely that hunting mortality is compensated for by relaxation of other forms of mortality. Since regulated sport hunting of cougars began, 3 main harvest strategies have been used (Dawn 2002). A **General Season** system, also called "open hunting" by Laundré and Clarke (2003), allows an unlimited number of cougars of either sex to be removed from the population during the hunting season. No restriction is placed on the number of hunters allowed. The only control over harvest is setting season timing and length. Vagaries of weather (adequate snow for tracking or deep snow preventing access) will often result in annual variation in harvest even if season timing and length remain constant. Under this strategy, hunting pressure and harvests will not be spread evenly over the hunt area.

Rather areas that are most easily accessible will be heavily hunted and others hunted little if at all. Topography and land ownership patterns may create refuges within the larger hunt area that can contribute young to support that segment of the population that is exposed to harvest. While general seasons may provide the greatest hunting opportunities to the largest number of hunters, managers will have only limited control over harvest level, composition and distribution.

Second, **Limited Entry** Programs control the number of hunters allowed to hunt a given area by limiting the number of licenses sold. Licenses are sold, either first come-first served until the supply is exhausted, or by way of a lottery. This system can be used to reduce and distribute hunters, thereby relieving pressure on areas where easy access increases the number of hunters (Murphy 1983). The strategy may also be of use where lower hunter densities are desirable such as in areas used heavily by the public for other activities. If the primary reason for such a season is biological, managers will need to understand the general relationship between the number of licenses sold and the number of cougars harvested to arrive at the number of licenses to be offered to meet population objectives. The number of cougars harvested will vary annually even when license numbers are held constant, because weather patterns, methods of take and hunter effectiveness will differ. The cost of license sales to the agency will increase if drawings are necessary to allocate the limited licenses.

The third strategy, **Quota** systems, set a legal limit on the number of cougars that may be harvested in a season or in a particular area. Harvest quotas are set for either total number of cougars, total number of females or, less frequently, total number of males. With total number quota seasons, hunting ends when a specified number of cougars are killed, irrespective of gender (and irrespective of age in some states) or when the season ends. With female sub-quotas the season closes when the female quota has been reached or at the end of the legal season, whichever occurs first. In some cases, the season may remain open for male-only harvest after the female quota has been reached. The quota system can be used to regulate distribution of hunting pressure, reduce or increase harvest or to tailor sex composition of the harvest, depending upon objectives. Quota systems will require that agencies develop a system whereby hunters can be notified when the quota is met. It is not uncommon for the quota to be exceeded because hunters harvest animals during the grace period. It is possible hunters are less selective of sex and age of cougars as the number of cougars harvested approaches the quota limit. Even experienced hunters may have difficulty determining the gender of younger cougars (Anderson and Lindzey 2000, Pierce and Bleich 2003).

When limited entry or quota systems are applied to influence the sex composition of the harvest, the objective is usually to protect the adult female segment of the population, thereby reducing the impact of harvest on the long-term productivity of the cougar population.

To promote sound research in service of management, we recommend:

1. Incorporate landscape thinking into cougar harvest strategies.

Cougars are best viewed and managed as widely dispersed but interacting metapopulations (Guideline 4.1). Management of any subpopulation influences—and is influenced by—management actions in adjacent subpopulations, and perhaps by actions in relatively remote subpopulations. In developing hunt recommendations, managers should consider:

- Cougars are highly mobile and distributed as *metapopulations* consisting of *source* and *sink* populations (terms defined in Guideline 4.1, implications discussed in 4.2 and throughout Chapter 3).
- Sink populations can be created by hunting pressure or predator reduction actions in areas that might otherwise be self-sustaining.
- Cougars disperse across large expanses to occupy areas far from their places of birth. This tendency has allowed cougars to repopulate areas that have been depleted, and to stabilize population sinks. Recovery of sinks is related to their connectivity to source populations. If connectivity is lost, this resilience will also be lost.
- High and sustained removals from a source can reduce dispersal from that source into dependent sinks. Modeling these relationships is difficult, perhaps impossible (Guideline 4.21). A conservative approach suggests that at least some source populations should be managed as refuges (Guideline 3.2).
- Harvest regulations applied to small units with boundaries that do not coincide with cougar populations may not accomplish intended objectives (Guidelines 3.1, 4.1).
- Successful harvest management may in some cases require cooperative management across state/provincial boundaries. It is not uncommon for states to cooperatively manage interstate ungulate populations.

2. Implement Zone Management or a related harvest strategy at the state level.

Two related approaches that acknowledge the need for a landscape approach to cougar management have been developed from long-term population studies: the zone management structure (Logan and Sweanor, 2001: 384-388,

Logan et al. 2003) and the metapopulation approach (Laundré and Clark 2003, Stoner and Wolfe 2003). Zone management recognizes the source and sink metapopulation structure of cougar populations and employs adaptive management. It partitions the state into relatively large zones with different population management objectives. Management in each zone is approached as an experiment, with its own objectives, hypotheses, and prescriptions. Monitoring is essential to allow managers to evaluate results and adjust their management strategies.

Logan and Sweanor (2001) recommend 3 zone categories: a) control zones, where reduction of cougar numbers is the objective; b) hunting zones, where management is directed toward sustaining populations to provide sport hunting opportunity; and c) refuge zones, where no hunting is allowed to manage for

KEN LOGAN

Sport hunting is the major source of human-caused mortality in cougar populations in the western United States.

reliable source populations and natural selection. The function of the refuge zones is to provide dispersing cougars for numeric and genetic augmentation of the control and hunting zones, and to increase the probability that selection processes will be more natural than man-caused. Refuge zones are also intended to dampen effects of management mistakes that might negatively impact cougar populations in the hunting zones, and to serve as reference areas in cougar research or monitoring designs (Logan and Sweanor 2001). New Mexico adopted a form of zone management in 1998, but allowed continued hunting of areas designated as refuge zones. Washington has recently adopted the concept of zone management, but without designated refuges.

The metapopulation approach proposed for southern Idaho was based on estimates of cougar numbers within sub-populations on scattered mountain ranges, some of which were considered to function as source populations and some as sinks. Laundré and Clark (2003) recommended closing more than half of cougar habitat to hunting, while permitting traditional hunting levels in others. They recommended that closed areas be large enough to contain source populations, and that hunting occur in those that functioned as sinks. In Utah, Stoner and Wolfe (2003) recommend that closed areas be commensurate in size and quality to sinks, and that spacing between them not exceed mean female dispersal distances.

If the management objective is to maintain harvest in sink areas, harvest levels cannot exceed immigration rates. Hunting small, isolated cougar populations may result in a high risk of extirpation.

3. Transition from general seasons toward limited entry or quota systems to achieve adaptive management objectives.

Although general seasons have worked well for many decades, and may still work in some regions, this approach fails to consider metapopulation structure. As roads and urbanization increasingly fragment even large landscapes dominated by public land, general seasons will become increasingly inappropriate. Thus agencies will need to transition into Limited Entry or Quota systems, or some other new approach that allows management objectives specific to each cougar management unit.

Use of limited entry or quota systems requires that cougar licenses be sold individually and not issued as an addition to other licenses. Data on harvest level, hunter numbers, and hunting effort are more efficiently obtained if hunters are required to obtain a cougar tag.

4. Monitor for harvest objectives and hunter acceptance.

Limited entry and quota systems involve unit-specific harvest objectives. Managers should monitor the harvest to ensure that these objectives are being met. At a minimum, this requires accurate data on the size and composition of the harvest.

Limited Entry and Quota systems are often used to protect part of the adult female segment of the population from harvest. The idea is that reducing competition among hunters (Limited Entry) or limiting the numbers of females taken (either system) will increase the harvest of males relative to females. In a recent comparison of cougar sport harvest strategies in the 10 western United States, Dawn (2002) found that the percentage of females in the harvest was 43% for general and quota systems, 40% in limited entry systems, and 38% in strategies that included female sub-quotas. These small differences do not provide compelling support for the hypothesis that limited entry systems increase hunter selectivity for males. However, Dawn (2002) reported statewide averages, pooling across units with differing objectives. Dawn (2002) also found that general harvest seasons resulted in lower harvests than limited entry or quota strategies. With the exception of Wyoming, the highest harvests occurred in states using female sub-quotas. These results suggest that restrictive strategies are at least potentially consistent with large harvests, but there were several potentially confounding factors. General seasons were most commonly being used shortly after the end of the bounty period, when cougar numbers were supposedly reduced throughout the western United States (Nowak 1976); more restrictive strategies have been implemented in recent decades, when the cougar population had apparently recovered. Clearly there are opportunities to investigate these relationships in a more rigorous manner.

The long-term success of limited entry and quota systems depends on hunter acceptance of the scheme. Therefore managers should regularly survey hunters, especially during the early years of transition away from general seasons, to determine how well they understand, accept, and comply with the regulations. If hunters feel deprived of the opportunity to hunt at all, or to hunt in favorite areas (often close to home) they may no longer feel a vested interest in the welfare of "their" local population. Hunter contribution to enforcement efforts may also be reduced. Most hunters are strong supporters of reasonable regulations if they are educated on the issues. Appropriate education should precede the transition away from general seasons, and continue afterward. Transparency in the development of regulations will probably result in fewer administrative or legal challenges.

5. Monitor for achievement of population objectives.

Meeting *harvest* objectives, such as "removal of no more than 15 adult females per year in Unit 1," as described in the previous Guideline, does not guarantee that the strategy also meets the manager's *population* objective, such as "ensure that Unit 1 remains a source population." It is expensive to monitor population objectives with sufficient precision (Guidelines 4.4 through 4.10), but we suggest that using several lines of evidence may suffice to detect a major failure. We recommend monitoring the sex-age composition of the harvest in all units annually (Guideline 4.9). Although this index has not been proven reliable, it has strong intuitive appeal, and the data are available for each management unit for the cost of compiling tag returns.

Because age-sex composition is hard to interpret on its own, we recommend using an additional index (Guideline 4.9) or population estimator (Guidelines 4.4 and 4.5) for a representative sample of cougar management units within the state or province, including units managed for different objectives (e.g., source, sink, refuge). It would be prohibitively expensive to collect such data in every unit. As a result, states might decide to monitor only a handful of units for the first few years, then evaluate whether changes are needed.

These recommended data are meaningless if they reside only in a stack of tag returns and survey report forms. *It is essential that these data be tabulated every year with an accompanying narrative that interprets the patterns both by management unit and state-/province-wide.* The key question to be addressed in the accompanying narrative is "Are these data consistent with a population that is meeting the population objective for that unit?" Because such analyses have not been attempted before, there are no rules for deciding what results indicate that a population is successfully functioning as a source, but we hope that marked failures will be easier to detect. For instance, if the index for the intended source population over a 5-year period resembles the downward trajectory of an intended sink, managers would want to list and evaluate all possible explanations and then adapt the management prescriptions accordingly.

6. Seasons should be timed primarily to protect females and young, and secondarily to meet hunter preferences.

Most states and provinces have laws that protect kittens and females with kittens. But it can be difficult to tell when a female has kittens because kitten tracks accompany their mother's tracks only 25% of the time, and females are located near their kittens only 67% of the time (Barnhurst and Lindzey 1989). Because hunters often will not know when a female has kittens, the hound-hunting seasons should avoid the months when defenseless young are most likely to be killed by hounds. Kittens are generally able to climb to avoid dogs at about 3 months of age, but kittens orphaned when they are 6 months old have a less than 5% chance of survival, and most die from starvation (Guideline 4.15).

Timing of seasons can facilitate individual cougar selection and success by hunters. For example, hound-hunting seasons during snow cover help many hunters to distinguish sex of cougars from their tracks, detect presence of kittens when possible, and to bay cougars in trees for closer inspections. Hunting with dogs should be timed to avoid other big game hunting seasons because other hunters often assume hounds are harassing the game animals they are attempting to hunt. This problem is somewhat self-limiting because most houndsmen avoid areas where their dogs risk being shot by other hunters.

7. Hound hunters can be more selective in harvesting cougars.

Compared to other methods of hunting cougars, hunting with hounds can be more selective of the sex and age of cougar harvested, increasing the achievement of harvest objectives. After Washington state made it illegal to hunt cougars with hounds, the total harvest remained the same. However, the median age of harvested cougars declined (females from 4.7 to 2.7, and males from 5.8 to 2.9 years), and the percentage of females in the harvest increased from 43% with hounds to 58% (Martorello and Beausoleil 2003). Less selective hunter harvest will be problematic for wildlife managers and should be considered when establishing harvest strategies.

Public opposition to hunting cougars with hounds is increasing. For example, 57% of Wyoming residents felt hunting with dogs should be eliminated (Wyoming Game and Fish 1997, Mountain Lion Management Plan). In Utah, 54% of rural and 63% of urban residents polled disapproved of the use of hounds to hunt cougars (Teel et al. 2002). Oregon and Washington have banned the use of hounds for hunting cougars. Some opposition has probably been fueled by the commercial nature of hound hunting, which benefits a small number of skilled houndsmen and guides, and by observations or rumors of unethical behavior of houndsmen and guides.

Hunters using hounds can be more selective of the cougar harvested, increasing the likelihood that management objectives will be achieved.

8. Sport hunting to benefit wild ungulate populations is not supported by the scientific literature.

Reducing cougar numbers through sport hunting is sometimes proposed to increase numbers of deer or elk, or to benefit an endangered ungulate population, such as desert bighorn sheep. Managers should carefully consider the wisdom and public acceptability of reducing cougar numbers simply to provide more ungulates for hunters to shoot. Such an effort should be undertaken with broad input from stakeholders. Even if there is support for the goal, managers should consider whether sport hunting is an effective tool that can reduce cougar numbers enough, and in the right locations, to benefit the ungulate populations.

Any effort to control cougars should be part of an effort that addresses all factors impacting the ungulate population. Increased cougar predation on a bighorn sheep population, for instance, may be driven by woody plant invasion (which provides cougar ambush sites and increases deer numbers, attracting cougars to the area) or predator subsidies in the form of calves. Isolation by roads may further impede immigration that could stabilize the bighorn population. Any cougar reduction should be undertaken in the context of an adaptive management process that addresses all these factors (Chapter 8).

9. Sport hunting has not been shown to reduce risk of attack on humans.

Sport hunting is occasionally proposed as a tool to reduce the risk that cougars will attack humans. There is no scientific evidence that sport hunting achieves this goal. In rare cases where a cougar exhibits dangerous behavior and needs to be removed, this job is best done by a professional to expeditiously track and kill the individual cougar, rather than via sport hunting.

Assuming that mortality from sport hunting is at least partially additive to other sources of mortality, hunting must reduce cougar density. Proponents of hunting use this reasoning to argue that sport hunting—by reducing cougar density—must also reduce risk of attack on humans. However, hunting may shift cougar population structure toward young animals, which are more likely than adult cougars to attack humans (Beier 1991). Furthermore, the public may not support efforts to reduce regional cougar populations in a questionable effort to reduce a minuscule risk.

Arguments for decreasing cougar density often focus on scenarios of cougars lurking near human homes and settlements. Because few cougars are more than 1 home range width from some sort of human settlement, this argument may be nothing more than a rhetorical device to promote regional hunting. Sport hunting of cougars near the densest human settlements is difficult because houndsmen are reluctant to hunt these areas (due to the risk that dogs will be killed on paved roads), and private landowners or local laws often prohibit hunting. Furthermore, although cougar attacks do occur close to human settlements, they do not seem to be concentrated there (Beier 1991). As described in the next guideline, sport hunting programs should be justified by honestly describing the likely benefits of the program.

10. Human attitudes must be considered in sport hunting programs.

As the human population in North America changes from rural to urban, attitudes towards cougars increasingly favor restrictions on cougar hunting. Where concerns of non-hunting groups were not adequately addressed, legislation or ballot initiatives have been used in places to override the authority of wildlife agencies (California, Washington, and Oregon). Public scrutiny of management policies, especially those that affect wildlife on public lands, has lead to an increase in the number of court actions filed against both state and federal agencies. Wildlife managers must recognize that the success of any program, including those for sport harvesting of cougars, will depend upon their ability to involve all interest groups (hunters, outfitters, conservationists, ranchers, and the general public) in the planning phase (Bailey 1984). Increasingly, managers are expected to provide evidence that a cougar population can sustain hunting, to disclose the manner in which population objectives are set, and to monitor results (Lindzey 1991).

Public attitudes will need to be considered in any cougar management program that includes sport hunting. If sport hunting is being used as a tool to meet other objectives, agencies need to provide evidence that hunting will achieve the objectives. If hunting is proposed solely as a recreational opportunity, agencies should state this clearly.

11. Develop cougar harvest strategies in a framework of adaptive management.

Cougar populations can sustain harvest rates of up to 20-30%, depending on sex and age composition of the harvest, and can recover rapidly from overexploitation (Chapter 4). However, we have much to learn about the sustainability of these rates, especially as habitats become altered. Accordingly, hunting programs should be designed to be evaluated as working hypotheses—with adequate data gathered on cougar harvest, survival, indices to cougar abundance or population estimates, and prey population trends—to provide reliable strategy evaluations.

In an adaptive management approach, measurable predictions about the outcome of a hunting prescription are made, success is evaluated by how well predictions are met, and the program is modified if needed to meet objectives. Our understanding of how cougar populations function and how they occupy the landscape has increased considerably during the last 3 decades. This new knowledge must be incorporated when planning cougar harvest strategies, with continued evaluation and refinement.

12. Pursuit seasons should be given cautious consideration.

Houndsmen often seek cougar hunting regulations that allow hound owners to work their dogs throughout the year. Some jurisdictions have approached this with "pursuit seasons" wherein cougars may be chased but not killed. Although popular with houndsmen, these seasons may not be accepted by the general public.

Although no definitive data exist regarding the impact of frequent chases on cougar, Harlow et al. (1992) documented changes in the physiological responses of cougars that were chased and treed multiple times ($n = 6$), compared to cougars chased only twice. These changes may have reflected an adaptive response to frequent chases or may have indicated a significant impact on their immune system, which may have resulted in reduced survival rates. Other perceived concerns include increased law enforcement problems, and risk of direct cougar deaths—especially killing of kittens.

CHAPTER 7

STRATEGIES TO MANAGE
COUGAR-HUMAN CONFLICTS

Maintaining a sustainable population of cougars will result in human-cougar encounters. The following guidelines may reduce the chance of a negative encounter and help agencies evaluate and respond to encounters. We suggest that interpretations of cougar behavior are a starting point for understanding observations and proposing management alternatives. These interpretations and alternatives should be modified as new information becomes available.

It is helpful to consider behaviors on a spectrum from *natural* to *habituated* to *overly familiar* to *nuisance* to *dangerous*, where successive terms indicate increasingly undesirable behavior. *Habituated* refers to frequent use of developed areas, campgrounds, trails, or roadsides by a cougar. Habituated cougars appear comfortable in the presence of humans. Although there are no rigorous studies documenting habituation of cougars to humans, the plausible scenario is that if a cougar frequently encounters humans and their artifacts without any negative consequence associated with such experiences, its tendency to avoid humans and human developments will wane over time. *Overly familiar* behavior is when a cougar purposefully approaches a human, or allows a human to approach it after the cougar has seen the human. A *nuisance* cougar is one that exhibits overly familiar behaviors more than once. *Stalking* is a natural behavior generally considered predatory and is characterized by a deliberate and (usually) slow approach from a moderately crouched posture, intense staring at and following of potential prey, holding the neck and head straight forward from the body, and holding ears up or slightly flattened. Stalking is considered dangerous when directed toward a human. *Dangerous* behavior is displayed aggression (non-defensive) toward humans expressed by postures, vocalizations, and actions communicating an intention to harm the individual at which they are directed. *Aggressive behaviors* may also be *defensive* if elicited by a perceived threat to itself, its young, or a food source, or when a cougar is surprised or harassed.

A hiking stick allowed this hiker to repel this cougar, and makes an effective deterrent.

Cougar attacks (intentional aggressive contacts) on humans are exceedingly rare, but have increased in recent decades and may still be increasing. Beier (1991) documented a total of 9 fatal attacks on 10 humans and 44 non-fatal attacks on 48 humans in the United States and Canada between 1890-1990. Most victims (66%) were unsupervised children or lone adults. Of the attacks, 30% were in or near (within sight of) developed areas. In 22 of 30 cases where pre-attack behavior of the human could be determined, the human did not see the cougar prior to physical contact. When the human did see the cougar approach, 4 humans ran, 3 simply watched the cougar, and 1 climbed a tree; none of these actions prevented the attack. Fitzhugh et al. (2003) report a total of 16 fatal and 92 non-fatal attacks from 1890-2003. Of those, 7 fatal and 38 non-fatal attacks occurred after Beier published his report, and 10 non-fatal attacks apparently were missed by Beier (1991). Increases in human encounters are likely due to a combination of factors, including reduction of cougar habitat, encroachment by a rapidly expanding human population into the remaining habitat, increasing recreation in cougar habitat, and possibly increases in cougar numbers or habituation.

Underweight or yearling cougars may have a propensity to attack humans. From limited data on offending cougars, Beier (1991) found that 42 percent (13 of 31) were under 2 years of age, and 57 percent (17 of 30) were underweight.

Building on Beier's (1991) summary, Torres et al. (1996) summarized (through 1995) the genders of cougars associated with attacks and found that both males and females are equally represented. In Big Bend National Park, Texas, sub-adults were the age group most likely to come into contact with humans (Ruth 1991). Cougars become independent from their mothers in their second year, and most disperse in search of new home ranges (Logan and Sweanor 2001). Their dispersal movements increase their probability of encounters with humans and human developments, and their inexperience and unfamiliarity with their environment may cause them difficulty in capturing wild prey. This combination of inexperience, unfamiliarity, and hunger may cause young cougars to have a higher percentage of negative encounters with humans. The period of learning and the investigation actions of a cougar may be one explanation for the curiosity that cougars have displayed toward humans. In addition, younger cougars may express a greater variation of behaviors toward humans, including a higher frequency of aggression.

A person's risk level varies depending on the location and conditions. For example, the risk of being attacked by a cougar within a large city is close to zero, while the estimated human risk within areas inhabited by wild cougars is higher. For example, along the eastern slope of the front range in Colorado, the risk of attack has been estimated at about 1 in 2,200,000 person-days (Halfpenny et al. 1991). Furthermore, in a given area where a cougar exhibits repeated unexpected or unusual behavior, the local risk is probably greater, and humans may be subjected to a level of risk that they do not expect. Cougar attacks occur more frequently during warmer months, a characteristic that Beier (1991) explained may be due to greater human activity in wildlands at those times. In the 20 years from 1970-1990 the risk of an attack increased fivefold, from 0.5 human attacks/year to 2.5/year. In the period 1990-2003, the risk of attack rose to 3.5 attacks/year. However, the per capita rate of attack may not have changed over the last 20 years. Mattson et al. (2003) suggest that not only cougar numbers, but also human knowledge, behavior, and distribution of human facilities influence the level and nature of human encounters with cougars.

Reports from Olympic National Park, Washington state (Patty Happe, Olympic National Park, personal communication), Yosemite National Park, California (Steve Thompson, Yosemite National Park, personal communication), and Big Bend National Park (Ruth 1991), suggest that cougars may become habituated to human developments and activities. Whether habituated or not, cougars may experiment with humans as potential prey (Aune 1991). There is no scientific evidence that habituation increases risk of attack.

Both innate and learned behaviors help cougars identify and attack prey, and respond to non-prey animals.

Predatory behavior in all species of wild and domestic cats is remarkably similar (Leyhausen 1979). Because cougars are so difficult to observe, much of our understanding about cougar behavior is inferred from research on other cat species. Felid behavior consists of innate and learned components. Innate behaviors are specific responses to certain stimuli, and are not significantly modified by environmental conditions during development of the individual animal. For example, running of a nearby, prey-sized animal may result in chasing and catching movements. Likewise, normally non-prey animals that are not too large and exhibit behaviors characteristic of prey may stimulate a predatory response. Learned behaviors are responses to stimuli that are adjusted to existing conditions (for example, prey types or habitat). Once a learned behavior develops it may be impossible to modify (Leyhausen 1979). For example, once a cougar learns that deer are prey, this may never change regardless of subsequent experiences.

In North America, deer and elk are the principal prey for cougars. However, small mammals are also taken, and may sustain young or injured cougars that lack the skill or strength to take large prey. Cougars may also be attracted to prey that have congregated in areas where humans have left an abundance of food (e.g., dump sites, hobby animal feeding stations, ungulate feeding sites).

Cougar kittens learn prey identification at least partially from their mother, but when on their own, they undoubtedly are faced with animals of the appropriate size about which they must determine prey suitability. Potential prey-animals' responses during encounters likely determine the young cougar's response (e.g., running elicits chasing; quick frightened movements and noises may cause stalking). Proper "positioning" of the prey item may also influence a cougar's response (e.g., the prey may appear more vulnerable to attack because it is lying down, smaller than the cougar, below a slope, or in a stance which tends to make the cougar "feel" larger).

Upon contact with another animal, a cougar identifies it as either prey or non-prey. Non-prey items may be the target of aggressive behavior (growling, hissing, charging, physical contact) if identified as a threat. A non-prey item encountered at particularly close range, or in close proximity to kittens or a food source, may evoke defensive actions. Attack may be the best form of defense for the cougar and therefore the elements of attacking and defensive behavior may be superimposed, giving the cougar the option of either launching an attack or running away (Leyhausen 1979).

The period of learning and the investigation actions of a cougar may be one explanation for the curiosity that cougars have displayed toward humans.

Leyhausen (1979) describes the prey's shoulder region as the usual area of attack. After the initial strike with a paw, a cat usually grasps with its teeth only if it meets with no resistance. If a victim struggles violently during an attack, the prey may be released followed by a repeat attack. It appears a prey item that becomes aggressive prior to or after a predatory attempt does not fit the cat's expectation of the prey and the attack may be broken off. Consequently, a person may break off a cougar's attack by fighting back.

Leyhausen (1979) described the facial expressions and head movements that may be particularly revealing of a cat's intended actions when it encounters another animal. Maintaining eye contact may restrain a cougar from attacking if the individual is regarded as a higher-ranking conspecific or as prey. If the individual is perceived as a social equal, however, an attack will more likely occur. Direct eye contact from prey may abruptly inhibit predatory action. If a cat stalking prey realizes it has been detected, it will immediately straighten up, "look around," and appear indifferent to the presence of the prey. Leyhausen suggests that this may serve to reduce the fight/flight response in the prey, allowing the cat another opportunity for attack without undue energy expenditures associated with a prolonged chase. In contrast, attack is often averted

Ears flat, fur out, tail twitching, with body and head low to the ground and rear legs "pumping" may precede an attack.

between social equals by gestures that interrupt contact (e.g., "looking around"). According to Leyhausen, these behaviors serve a double function. If cat A averts its gaze, it is reducing its own provocation to either attack or escape, and is also interrupting the same stimulus effect in cat B. The one severing contact is actively avoiding being provoked to attack or escape.

We offer the following principles and guidelines to help managers evaluate and manage the risk of cougar attacks on humans:

1. Behaviors may be interpreted as indicators of the risk of a predatory attack.

Cougar behaviors may differ for a confrontation with a non-cougar compared to a confrontation with another cougar, and certain body positions and movements may be characteristic of these behaviors. *Avoidance* (flight or hiding by the cougar) indicates no interest in further contact with the animal. *Indifference* is reflected in a lack of attention, or various body movements and positions not directed toward the non-cougar.

Curiosity may be expressed by various behaviors and changing body positions including following. Intense staring coupled with hiding behavior may indicate that the animal is *assessing the likelihood that an attack will succeed.* At the stage of curiosity or assessment, activity of the human (or other potential prey) may be particularly important. *Pre-attack* behaviors of crouching, tail twitching,

Table 7.1. Interpretation of cougar behaviors, arranged in order of increasing risk to a human interacting with the cougar. Managers should not rely solely on these behaviors to assess risk, because cougars are ambush predators whose behavior usually is not observed before an attack on a human.

Observation	Interpretation	Human Risk
Opportunistically viewed at a distance.	Secretive	Low
Flight, hiding.	Avoidance	Low
Lack of attention, various movements not directed toward person.	Indifference, or actively avoiding inducing aggression	Low
Various body positions, ears up; may be shifting positions; intent attention; following behavior.	Curiosity	Low–provided human response is appropriate.
Intense staring; following and hiding behavior.	Assessing success of attack	Moderate
Hissing, snarling, vocalization.	Defensive behaviors. Attack may be imminent	Moderate, depending on distance to animal
Crouching; tail twitching; intense staring; ears flattened like wings; body low to ground; head may be up.	Pre-attack	High
Ears flat, fur out; tail twitching; body and head low to ground; rear legs "pumping."	Imminent attack	Very high and immediate

intense staring, and flattening of the ears may be preceded by stalking. We speculate that aggressive action by a human at these 3 stages has maximum likelihood of teaching the cougar to avoid humans. If the interpretations suggested in Table 7.1 are correct, then the cougar is in "learning mode" and would be maximally teachable at this time.

Defensive behavior may include hissing, snarling, and other vocalizations that make the cougar conspicuous, and communicate to the confronted animal that it is viewed as a threat to the safety of the cougar, a food source, or its young. Females with kittens may be most likely to exhibit defensive responses. Although defense of kittens or a kill was not implicated in any of the 53 attacks tabulated by Beier (1991), a recent attack in California (2004) may have been the result of a cougar defending a kill. Researchers in New Mexico approached to within 50 m of radio-collared cougars on 172 occasions, and threat responses (e.g., vocalizations, ears back and down, approach, and/or charge) were elicited 16 times (Sweanor et al. in press.) The majority of the threat responses were made by mothers with nursing ($n = 11$) or weaned ($n = 3$) kittens.

Leyhausen (1979) refers to behaviors as representing a "momentary hierarchy." That is, almost all of these "behaviors" can occur in attack or defense, but in the described "moods" it is "easiest" to bring about a given response. Considering these behaviors as a continuum (Table 7.1) may be useful in evaluating cougar observations and in assessing potential risk to a human encountering a cougar (E. L. Fitzhugh, University of California Cooperative Extension, Davis, personal communication). However, cougars are ambush predators, and many of these behaviors will occur out of view and thus often will not be useful cues to an impending attack.

2. Management should be directed at avoiding encounters and reducing chances of attack.

The progression from cougar observation to an attack may be abrupt, and most attacks occur without prior interactions that convey the impending attack. Cougars can and do kill humans, albeit rarely. Within areas that support cougar populations, there is no way to prevent all cougar encounters or attacks, and humans are accepting risk as a consequence of using these wildlands just as automobile users accept 37,000 deaths per year as a consequence of having the convenience of using motorized vehicles (USDT 2004). The challenge for managers is to modify human activities and behaviors to reduce this risk. It should be much more effective for humans to modify their own behavior than it is for humans to modify cougar behavior. The following guidelines greatly reduce the risk to those who visit or live in cougar country.

a) When hiking, hike in groups. Unsupervised children are most vulnerable to attacks, so children should be kept within view of adults at all time, and very small children within arms' reach. It may also help to make enough noise to avoid surprising a cougar.

In Beier's (1991) analysis, the majority of victims (66%) were unsupervised children or lone adults. Fitzhugh et al. (2003) indicated solitary people were 3 times as likely as groups to encounter or be attacked by a cougar. Groups of 5 or more appeared relatively secure against attack. Fitzhugh et al. (2003) suggests that the likelihood of a cougar being close to, and subsequently encountering, humans decreases with group size; however, once the cougar is close, the probability of attack is not clearly related to group size. Attacks on larger groups typically involved groups of children.

b) Closely supervise children whenever they are playing outdoors in cougar habitat. Do not allow them to play in vegetation that could provide hiding or stalking cover for cougars. When possible, design landscaping or remove

This cougar made its appearance during a dry Arizona summer. Cougar observations commonly occur during the day and in open, highly visible areas.

vegetation to eliminate hiding cover near children's play areas. Make it difficult for a cougar to approach unseen.

Cougars use vegetative cover and terrain to approach prey and seek dense overstories and understories when resting, stalking, and feeding on prey (Laing and Lindzey 1991, Logan and Irwin 1985).

c) Try to avoid activities that place children outside at dusk or after dark (when cougars are most active). Hikers should also be made aware of, and accept, increased risk at dawn and dusk.

d) Close off open spaces below porches or decks to eliminate access to hiding places for cougars.

e) Do not attract deer by providing food (e.g., corn, apples), or landscaping with plants palatable to deer.

f) Do not let pets roam, or leave pet food outside where it can attract wild animals. Pets should be brought inside at night or provided with a completely enclosed kennel, including a roof. Hobby animals should be placed in enclosed sheds or barns at night.

This startled and curious cougar retreated when the hikers shouted and waved their arms.

Cougars regularly prey on domestic dogs and cats where residential areas invade cougar habitat (Aune 1991, Beier and Barrett 1993, Torres et al. 1996). Domestic animals that are left unprotected may "bait" cougars into human communities, putting the pet, the pet's owner, and the cougar at greater risk for a negative encounter. Secure enclosures effectively protected hobby animals (chickens, alpacas) from depredation by cougars in southern California (L. Sweanor, Wildlife Health Center, University of California, Davis, personal communication). Young cougars that are still investigating their environment and learning about potential prey items and what is safe to be around may be most likely to attempt to kill unprotected pets and livestock.

g) Managers should encourage homeowners to take the precautions listed above to create a relatively safe zone around their homes and neighborhoods.

h) In residential areas and developed recreational sites (car-accessible picnic areas, car-accessible campgrounds, playgrounds) within cougar habitat, managers should post signs to inform visitors of potential cougar presence, and appropriate defensive actions (Guidelines 1 through 3, this chapter).

Table 7.2. Some of the measures, with supporting information, that humans can take during an encounter to prevent injury.

Recommendations	Supporting Information
Keep children under close control, and in view. Pick up small children immediately if you encounter a cougar. Do not hike alone.	60% of victims have been unsupervised children or lone adults.
Do Not Run.	Running and quick movements may stimulate chasing and catching response.
Stand. Wave your arms. Raise jacket over your head. Appear as large as possible. Move to higher ground if nearby. Throw sticks, rocks, or other objects if within reach and accessible without bending too low.	Prey size, vulnerability, and "positioning" influences cougar response.
Avoid dead animals and never approach kittens. Talk calmly. Back away.	Non-prey may be attacked if viewed as a threat.
Maintain eye contact. Do not look away. But if cougar appears agitated use peripheral vision to keep track of its location.	Eye-to-eye contact often restrains large cats. Direct eye contact from prey may inhibit predatory action.
Be alert to your surroundings.	Cats exploit all vantage points/cover when investigating prey.
If attacked, fight back. Humans have successfully deterred attacks by becoming aggressive.	A cat grasps with its teeth only if it meets with no resistance. Violently struggling prey may be released.
Secure pets and hobby animals in predator-proof enclosures between dusk and dawn. Keep pets on leashes and off trails in the backcountry.	Domestic prey animals may sustain cougar populations at unnaturally high levels.
Keep garbage under control to avoid attracting raccoons, skunks, etc. Do not feed pets outside and remove extra feed from domestic animal pens. Do not feed deer and wild turkeys.	Cougars may be attracted to concentrations of potential prey.
A cougar that treats humans as prey is a public safety threat.	Once a learned behavior develops it may not be possible to modify this behavior.
Cougars that enter yards or campsites to kill pets may be candidates for removal. Keep pets under control.	Once a learned behavior develops it may not be modifiable.

The recommendations above will not prevent all aggressive encounters. In the event of such an encounter, humans can increase their chances of avoiding an attack if they respond appropriately (Table 7.2). Perhaps most important, children should be protected during a cougar encounter. Immediately upon encountering a cougar, adults should bring children close into a tight group and pick up any small children. Adults should remain upright, face the cougar, and act aggressively (e.g., shout, throw rocks and sticks). The adult's goal is to convince the cougar that humans are dominant and a danger to cougars. If possible, the group should slowly back away to avoid communicating to the cougar that the group is a threat. If the cougar follows, the group should continue its aggressive behavior. If an attack occurs, victims should fight back.

Fitzhugh et al. (2003) examined 16 fatal and 92 non-fatal attacks that met the validity requirements established by Beier (1991), and another 32 alleged fatal and 84 alleged non-fatal attacks that failed to meet Beier's criteria. They also analyzed 155 accounts of close-proximity, behavioral interactions between humans and cougars that did not result in attacks. They concluded that noise might be an effective deterrent especially if repeated or prolonged. A single warning gunshot seemed less effective. Yelling and screaming were more effective than gunshots at deterring a cougar. Charging a cougar also appeared to help. They documented 6 accounts where the victim either charged the cougar and fought with it, or engaged in mock lunges toward the cougar. In all 6 cases the cougar backed down or left the area.

MIKE FONTAINE

Intense staring and following behavior may represent a moderate risk of attack.

3. Land management agencies should promote public education and outreach.

Education is basic to minimizing negative encounters between people and cougars. Many people have little knowledge about cougars or how to live and recreate safely in cougar country. Some state wildlife agencies, land management agencies and nongovernment organizations have developed educational pamphlets that provide the public with this information. We encourage wider distribution of these pamphlets. In areas where the probability of human-cougar conflicts is greatest, public workshops and use of other media (e.g., newspapers, television, radio) may be appropriate.

People who live and recreate in cougar country should make an effort to inform themselves about cougars, appropriate human behaviors, and risks. A useful pocket guide with basic facts and advice is *Lion Sense* (previously published as *Mountain Lion Alert*) by Steven Torres (2004). Local communities should be encouraged to form their own associations, where information can be obtained and distributed to new homeowners about behaviors and husbandry practices that could reduce conflicts.

4. Managers should be proactive rather than reactive.

Developing educational programs for human users of wildlands, procedures to identify and manage nuisance or dangerous cougars, and contingency plans to respond to an attack are activities best done prior to an attack or near-attack. For example, failing to evaluate reports of overly familiar cougars could result either in failure to recognize a potential threat to public safety, or the unwarranted removal of harmless cougars. Similarly, if an attack occurs, a contingency plan can help a manager collect the necessary evidence and remove the offending animal promptly. Such advance planning also maximizes our ability to learn from experience to prevent future attacks.

Contingency plans should include development of agreements with local or state entities that have the ability to selectively remove cougars. Having a network of qualified trackers, trappers, houndsmen, and sharpshooters can save precious hours in a crisis. The United States Department of Agriculture, Wildlife Services provides these services through agreements with state and local agencies. Managers of lands that contain cougars and their habitat should develop these contacts before encounters and/or attacks occur. Coordinate closely with local, state, and other federal agencies, and assign specific responsibilities to ensure successful implementation of the plan.

MOUNTAIN LION OBSERVATION FORM
REDWOOD NATIONAL AND STATE PARKS

Recorder Information
Name:_____
Duty Station:_____
Phone Number:_____
Date of RPT.:_____
Time of RPT.:_____

Please record the following information for all mountain lion observations. **At a minimum, record the observer's name(s) and telephone number** so that a follow-up can occur to obtain further information as necessary.

OBSERVER INFORMATION:

NAME(S): _____   _____

PHONE: (h)____ / _____ (w) ____ / _____   (h)____ / _____ (w) ____ / _____

ADDRESS: _____   ADDRESS: _____
CITY/STATE: _____ ZIP: _____   CITY/STATE: _____ ZIP: _____
ADULT: _____ # CHILD: _____ AGE OF CHILDREN: _____
TOTAL # PEOPLE:_____ PETS(# and type):_____
OTHER OBSERVERS:_____
(Include name, phone, address, age and sex)

OBSERVATION INFORMATION:
DATE/TIME OF OBS.: _____(AM/PM) **EXACT LOCATION:** _____
_____
(Name of road, trail, site; distance to nearest landmark, etc.)

SUMMARY OF INCIDENT:_____
_____
(Attach additional pages if necessary)

DESCRIPTION OF LION:
TAIL LENGTH (in inches): _____
WEIGHT (in pounds): _____
CONDITION:_____(e.g.. healthy, thin, if injured describe)
PHYSICAL MARKINGS OR SCARS:_____(please describe)
OVERALL BODY COLOR:_____
(Spotted, blond, light brown, med/dark brown, black, other, unknown)

ADDITIONAL INFORMATION
(OPTIONAL FOR DISTANT SIGHTINGS, PLEASE COMPLETE IF LION WAS IN CLOSE PROXIMITY)
BEHAVIORAL INFORMATION: *(see behaviors listed below)*

PERSON(S) ACTIVITY at time of observation *:_____
MOUNTAIN LION(S) ACTIVITY at time of observation **:_____
PERSON(S) RESPONSE to lion (describe in detail) *:_____
MOUNTAIN LION(S) RESPONSE to person(s) actions (describe in detail) **:_____
MOUNTAIN LION BEHAVIORAL/POSTURE SIGNS ***:_____
OBSERVER'S INTERPRETATION of the encounter:_____
(What did they think happened? Did they feel the lion was threatening or aggressive?)

Figure 7.1. Cougar incident report form utilized by Redwood National and State Parks.

* **Human activity and response examples:** on/off road/trail, driving, walking, hiking, running, standing, sitting, crouched, lying down, camping, stopped, fled, stood, faced animal, quiet, spoke to it, shouted, waved arms, threw things.

** **Lion activity and response examples:** standing, walking, running toward/away from person(s), sitting, crouched, lying down, hiding, feeding, with cubs, ignored, watched intently or casually, "charged".

*** **Lion behavioral/posture signs:** unknown, crouched, facing toward/away, moved/stalked closer, ears back/forward, teeth bared, growled, tail quiet/lashing, rear legs pumping, body low to ground, head low to ground, intense staring, looked away.

DURATION OF INCIDENT: _____ CLOSEST DISTANCE *(in feet)*: _____
                    (How long was lion in view)   *(Observer to lion)*

HABITAT:

_____
                (Vegetation type: old-growth, 2nd-growth, oak woodland, prairie, riparian, etc.)

OTHER INFORMATION: *(Example: smelly food/garbage present, nearby prey kill, photographs, videotapes)*

_____

RELIABILITY OF OBSERVATION: 1   2   3   4   5
                                Highly reliable   Highly questionable

RELIABILITY BASED ON: _____

SUBMIT AS SOON AS POSSIBLE TO: (Names, addresses, and phone numbers)

_____

(This section for wildlife branch use only)

Lion age	Summary of Interaction	Management Action
1. Kitten	1. Scat	1. No action
2. Sub adult	2. Track	2. Post area
3. Adult	3. Sighting	3. Monitoring
4. Unknown	4. Recurring sighting	4. Increase monitoring
	5. Encounter	5. Aversive conditioning
	6. Near attack	6. Close area
	7. Other(describe)	7. Relocation
		8. Removal

Follow up phone call(s) made _____
(Y/N, date, initials)

Entered into wildlife database _____
(Record #, date, initials)

UTM coordinates _____

OTHER INFORMATION:
_____
_____

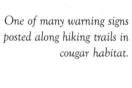

One of many warning signs posted along hiking trails in cougar habitat.

Wildlife and land managers should seek legal advice when considering actions to deal with potential human-cougar incidents and be aware that legal liability, stemming from incidents and human injury or property damage, may vary from state to state. Many states have enacted recreational use statutes to protect private landowners, and torts claims acts to protect public land managers from liability associated with an accident or injury suffered by recreationists. Ultimately, of course, a court may decide the applicability of statutes to any given situation and decide who or what agency is responsible for events that occur on their land. Many courts have required actual knowledge of a dangerous condition, that an injury could result from that condition, and that the agency took no action in the face of this knowledge before liability is assessed.

In general, public agencies do not have a legal obligation to warn visitors of what are obvious hazards associated with a given area. They do, however, have a legal obligation to inform the public of known dangers, and a responsibility to warn visitors of, or eliminate, "hidden" hazards. It is appropriate to post public information explaining that an area supports cougars in their natural habitat, the potential risks, and what to do if a cougar is observed. We see no reason for a manager to alert the public to sightings of cougars exhibiting normal behavior, nor to close such areas to the public. However, if a nuisance cougar (as defined previously) is in an area and no action is taken to either remove the cougar, close the area, or warn all visitors (of the exact danger), the agency could be found liable should an attack occur. In contrast, if an attack by a wild cougar (first attack) was not expected, there would probably be no liability (R. Mihan,

Solicitor, Department of Interior, Oakland, CA, personal communication). In these types of incidents occurring on public lands, there will probably be no liability unless the animal is no longer considered to be wild, having become "semi-domesticated." If injury results from this type of animal, the agency could be found liable (Mangus 1991).

5. Development patterns that increase human-cougar encounters should be discouraged.

Increased human encroachment into cougar habitat appears to be the major cause of increased cougar attacks on humans (Torres et al. 1996). In Redwood National and State Parks, California (1995), researchers found that, at the landscape scale, cougars used human-influenced areas (e.g., roads) less than expected (Meinke 2004) and while activities and movements during high visitor use seasons did not change, individual cougars modified their behaviors to avoid interacting with humans (Ellingson 2003). Increasing human development and density can overwhelm this "tendency" of wild cougars to avoid humans. County planning agencies may thus be important for managing cougar encounters over the long term. However, managers of parks and other wildlands also can profoundly affect encounters by choosing locations for developments, and by the way they concentrate or disperse visitors. For instance, placing trails in the best cougar habitat, and shuttling visitors in trams to both ends of that trail, is certain to maximize the chance of encounter between humans and cougars. Although we do not know how much habituation contributes to attacks, such a management practice would also be a recipe for encouraging cougars to habituate to humans.

Planning and environmental compliance documents (such as National Environmental Policy Act [NEPA] documents) should specifically evaluate whether implementing the proposal is likely to increase cougar-human encounters. State, county, and local jurisdictions that establish zoning and influence development patterns could benefit from considering how growth and expansion may influence interactions with humans.

6. Develop protocols to document and investigate reports of overly familiar, nuisance, or aggressive behavior by cougars.

Any agency that may be involved in a cougar-human conflict should create a cougar incident report form that will be available to all personnel who may need to respond to an incident. An example is provided in Figure 7.1. The officer who responds to the complaint should complete the form and make an initial determination of the response that may be necessary.

Table 7.3. Suggested protocol in decision-making process as related to single or multiple occurrences of behaviors in the risk categories defined in Table 7.1. See Guideline 7 for details.

Risk category: Specific behavior - number of occurrences	Recommended type of response	Recommended management actions
Low risk – single occurrence	Wait and see.	Continue or initiate public education.
Low risk – multiple occurrences	Take appropriate action. Evaluate circumstances of observations.	Post warning signs. Consider use of hazing. Consider database for observations.
Moderate risk. Deliberate approach (curiosity) – single occurrence.	Take appropriate action. Evaluate conditions leading to approach.	Post warning signs.Try to mark and monitor animal. Consider use of hazing. Map observations and document observations and management in database.
Moderate to high risk – multiple occurrences.	Take appropriate action. Evaluate conditions leading to approaches. Evaluate removal.	Post warning signs, or close area. Increase education effort. Patrol area with loaded firearm to kill cougar if perceived as dangerous, or haze if perceived as curious.
High risk: Near attack – single occurrence.	Take immediate action; Evaluate if behavior was predatory or defensive. Evaluate removal.	Post warning signs, or close area. Increase education effort. If decision is to remove, patrol area with loaded firearm to kill cougar.
High risk: nonfatal attack – single occurrence.	Take immediate action. Evaluate if attack was defensive.	Secure victim. Post warning signs and close area. Secure incident scene, contact Wildlife Services, and kill the cougar. Contact the media.
High risk: Fatal attack – single occurrence.	Take immediate action.	Close area. Secure incident scene, contact Wildlife Services, and kill the cougar. Assist and support victim's family. Contact the media.

A sighting of a cougar exhibiting normal behavior, or cougar sign, within cougar habitat do not indicate an immediate threat to human safety, and no investigation is warranted. If habituated, overly familiar, or nuisance behavior is alleged, the investigating official should carefully assess the credibility of the witness, keeping in mind that more than 75% of cougar sightings may be erroneous (Beier and Barrett 1993). The investigator should avoid asking leading questions ("Did it have a long tail? Did it growl?") and instead ask for details ("Describe the animal's size, color, and shape. What did it do? How far was the animal from you and from other landmarks like a road?"). The next step is to look for tracks or other indicators that a cougar was actually involved in the reported incident.

Most reported cougar sightings received by managers and researchers involve some other animal misidentified as a cougar (Beier and Barrett 1993). Furthermore, few observers provide the sort of detailed description (Table 7.1) that would allow a manager to interpret behavior. Managers need to develop clear but flexible guidelines on how reports should be handled, what types of cougar behavior will elicit certain types of management responses, and how targeted animals will be handled. Reported information should be entered into a database.

7. Level of response should be determined in advance.

Many agencies already have policies outlining steps to be taken in response to wildlife-human conflicts. Guidelines (Hofstra 1995a) for reacting to cougar encounters in national park units (Moorhead and Hofstra 1995, Hofstra 1995b) are summarized below. Response should be guided by a review of the circumstances surrounding observations, encounters, and incidents and will depend on the level of risk involved. Suggested management actions are summarized in Table 7.3.

Low risk sightings should be expected in any area where cougars reside and they are often viewed by outdoor recreationists as an exceptional experience. These require no management response; managers may wish to tabulate the reports. *Moderate risk* sightings involve cougars displaying abnormal behavior. As few as 2 incidents of overly familiar behavior by what is likely to be by the same individual cougar may warrant removal of the cougar, especially if the human threw rocks or acted aggressively in the first encounter. Educational materials should encourage visitors to act aggressively even to apparently "curious" cougars. If visitors are informed that the second incident could be fatal for the cougar, they may be more likely to heed the advice to "educate" curious cougars. Dealing with observations of "curiosity" (Table 7.1) in cougars may be particularly important, especially if this behavior represents a period of special receptivity to learning. Hazing, or scaring the animal away in the immediate situation, may be effective in precluding habituation. Slingshots, cracker shells, throwing rocks and sticks, or chasing with dogs from a specific area are examples of hazing.

We encourage removal in preference to aversive conditioning for any animal that clearly exhibits overly familiar behavior more than once. For borderline "curious" behavior, a manager may wish to consider aversive conditioning, but should be aware that there are no studies confirming its effectiveness. In one case, a cougar was shot with rock salt at close range after a near-attack; it exhibited aggressive behavior 2 weeks later and had to be removed (Beier 1991). If a cougar is judged dangerous to humans, it should be removed. Assistance from those organizations with whom arrangements have been previously established (see Guideline 5, this chapter) should be solicited.

The individual(s) reporting the sightings should be advised of the potential danger as well as measures they should take to reduce the chance of an incident (e.g., hike in a different area). Warnings should be posted, and a temporary closure imposed, until personnel can investigate and determine the level of danger. When unacceptable cougar behavior is reported, the agency responsible for cougar management should assist in the investigation.

High Risk incidents are considered an immediate threat to human safety. In cases where humans are clearly threatened, a closure should be imposed and the situation fully investigated. The responding officer should notify his immediate supervisor, as well as the state wildlife agency, of the situation. Witnesses to the incident should be interviewed to help determine: whether the cougar's behavior was predatory or defensive; whether or not it was cornered or accompanied by young; if it followed, stalked or chased the human; its physical condition; and whether it was surprised.

Following a near attack (i.e., where a cougar advances toward a human at close range, Beier 1991) that was not preceded by multiple approaches, warnings should be posted by the land manager to indicate that cougars have been encountered at close range in the area. The manager is then faced with evaluating whether the cougar's approach was predatory or defensive. All of the circumstances surrounding the incident must be evaluated carefully, especially whether the cougar may have been prompted to defensive action. Closing an area to public use during this period of evaluation is recommended. If it is determined that: 1) the near-attack has followed multiple observations of curiosity behavior or multiple approaches, 2) the possibilities of kittens or a kill

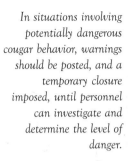

In situations involving potentially dangerous cougar behavior, warnings should be posted, and a temporary closure imposed, until personnel can investigate and determine the level of danger.

have been eliminated, and 3) the area is in or near a developed or front country area, the cougar should be euthanized.

Removal includes relocating offending cougars to a captive facility, or euthanizing them. Removal should not be considered a way to eliminate risk of attack, because cougars will remain in the area as part of the ecosystem (Fitzhugh 1988, Eberhardt 1977). The decision to kill a cougar is a serious matter, and usually receives negative public reaction. However, euthanasia is the only feasible alternative when managers feel that a significant threat to human safety exists.

8. We recommend that agencies determine the feasibility of, and their tolerance for, area closures and cougar removal before proposing them to resolve a specific situation.

Area closures prevent public interference during investigations and management activities such as hazing or cougar removal. They also allow time for a kill to be consumed, and for kittens to be weaned or moved by a female. If an area is closed to evaluate a potential public safety risk following a moderate to high risk occurrence (Table 7.3), it is recommended that the area be patrolled by trained, armed personnel when possible. These personnel should be authorized to kill the cougar if appropriate in their judgment, but should be trained to evaluate the risk of certain cougar behaviors (Table 7.1), or accompanied by staff with these skills. This will help preclude the killing of harmless animals yet allow for prompt removal of dangerous ones. If the investigator notes a kill within 5 m, or kittens within 20 m, of the incident, he/she may conclude that the cougar was not initiating a predatory attack. Otherwise, a cougar should be shot if exhibiting imminent attack or pre-attack behavior (Table 7.1). The area should be reopened to the public only after the investigation is over and the offending animal is no longer present. If the offending animal was never removed and the area is reopened, the public should be notified of the potential risk.

Relocation to wildlands is generally considered an ineffective management tool for most cougar-human incident situations. Killing of a cougar may be preferable to relocation to an area already occupied by cougars, as only the local population from which the animal is removed is affected. If the animal is a young, dispersing cougar (most typical of those involved in human encounters) it has already been continuously interacting and competing with residents and other transients. It could be argued that the effects of interacting with a new, "receiving" resident population may not be significant. However, the logistics of moving a cougar to a new location may be quite difficult. Obtaining permission of various state and local agencies, adjacent private and public landowners/managers, and dealing with issues of future liability may ultimately limit the feasibility of relocation. Research has documented that the distance a cougar must be removed from its territory to preclude its return may exceed 480 km (Ruth et al. 1998). Young cougars that do not have an established territory are the best candidates for translocation (Ruth et al. 1998); however, there is the risk they would continue their undesirable behavior and again find themselves interacting with humans. Where translocations have been evaluated, survival rates have been low, and movement patterns unpredictable (Ruth et al. 1998). The density and composition of the receiving population and habitat quality at the release site may also influence the success of translocations.

Plans for responding to a dangerous cougar should be made in advance. For example, if a non-target cougar is captured, how will it be released to ensure the safety of both cougar and trapper? If the target animal is a lactating female, what efforts will be made to locate kittens, and how will they be handled? Are there holding and transport facilities available? Who, specifically, will be assigned to oversee holding and transport, and are they capable of dealing with whatever emergencies might arise? Are contingencies established to handle injured cougars and/or humans? If a decision is made to kill a cougar because of unacceptable public risk, it must be accomplished in a professional, efficient, and humane manner. The most important consideration is to ensure that the correct animal is killed, and to collect evidence to let the public know that the correct animal was killed. A target animal must be identified by distinctive or unique tracks, coloration, or physical characteristics. When possible, these unique characteristics should be identified before capture is attempted.

9. Public agencies should establish their level of tolerance for various cougar behaviors in developed and remote areas.

Managers need to determine what behaviors will trigger removal of a cougar. In a highly developed area, multiple observations of a single animal exhibiting "curiosity" behavior might be sufficient. In more remote areas, 1 or 2 incidents of "assessing success" behavior might be tolerated, but 2 or 3 such incidents might trigger removal, especially if the humans responded aggressively. Most managers will have different thresholds for a given type of behavior near a camp frequented by school age children, along a trail, near a parking lot, or in the backcountry. In the absence of evidence that a cougar attack was a defensive response, all cougars involved in a human attack should be killed. Managers may also consider "curiosity" and "assessing success" as predatory in nature or at least representing precursor indications that predatory behavior toward humans could follow. As few as 1 or 2 near-attacks may be considered a threshold where removal is warranted. Managers will have to determine the point where action toward the cougar is warranted given individual circumstances. If a predatory action is initiated by a cougar toward a human, it is unlikely that the intended victim will observe the cougar immediately before the attack.

This cougar was tracked and killed within hours of attacking two people in Orange County, California in 2004. Investigators used bags to preserve any material present on the animal's head and paws before removing it from the scene. A sign in the immediate background reads, "Warning: Mountain lion country."

CALIFORNIA DEPARTMENT OF FISH AND GAME

10. Agencies should determine, and formalize, their response to a cougar attack on a human.

Most wildlife and law enforcement personnel have little experience handling cougar attacks because of their rarity. To reduce the confusion and the chance for serious mistakes, agencies should consider developing a standard protocol for handling cougar attacks. Few law enforcement officials who may be called to the site of a human attack or fatality have been trained to identify a cougar attack. Similarly, many non-law enforcement resource agency personnel are not trained how to protect and secure a crime scene. Consequently, resource and law enforcement agencies should communicate, via training sessions, and determine in advance how they will coordinate investigations of human injuries and fatalities in wild lands.

When an attack occurs, the victim's safety must be the top priority. Obtain a detailed report on the circumstances surrounding the attack from the victim, if possible, and all witnesses. If the decision is made to pursue and kill the offending cougar, several actions must be taken immediately. The attack site should be treated as a crime scene. An area at least 100 m in radius around the attack site should be secured against public entry to preserve evidence (e.g., drag lines, tracks, the victim's clothing). A secondary site outside the attack site should be established as a command post, but only essential, authorized personnel should be allowed into the attack site and then through only 1 entrance. In case of a human fatality, investigators other than those pursuing the animal will necessarily be allowed into the area. Investigators will have to confirm, for example, that this is not a homicide. Investigators should secure and label all evidence such as clothing, objects used for defense, or any items that may have the attacking animal's DNA, (e.g., saliva, hair, or blood on or near the victim). If the victim is dead, investigators should ensure that an appropriate representative is present at the autopsy to gather this needed information.

Pursuit of the cougar does not have to wait for the entire investigation to be completed or for the body to be removed. The faster that action is taken to pursue the cougar, the better the chances of a successful removal. If the cougar is still at the site, it should be killed immediately. In case of human fatality, replace the victim's body with another attractant (e.g., deer carcass), remove unnatural material such as flagging, and station a sharpshooter or set snares at the site in case the cougar returns to the site of the kill. If the cougar has left the site, methods for capture may include cage traps, neck and leghold snares, or hounds that trail and tree the cougar. All of these activities should be assigned to professionals (e.g., Wildlife Services, other experienced houndsmen or trappers). Airspace around the kill site should be restricted so that news crews in helicopters do not disrupt the trailing efforts made to catch the offending cougar. Live capture provides an opportunity to examine the animal prior to euthanasia and consequently make a better determination of whether the captured animal is the actual offender.

If the cougar is to be destroyed, avoid shooting it in the head. To avoid any contamination, protective gloves and a facemask should be worn when handling the carcass. Wrap paper, then plastic, bags over the head and paws, and place the entire carcass in a body bag. Carry, do not drag, the carcass from the site. The lead agency should take the carcass to the appropriate laboratory for necropsy.

Preserve all tracks. Even if a forensic investigation is taking place, make people aware of the importance of preserving this critical piece of evidence. Capturing the offending individual animal in these situations is critical. Tracks must be preserved so that tracking hounds can capture the cougar. Try to begin pursuit of the cougar with hounds within 6 hours of the incident if possible. After approximately 24 hours, cougar tracks and scent become less discernible, making it significantly more difficult to identify the correct animal. Keep all involved employees or other witnesses available until they have been questioned by criminal investigators and those involved in the capture of the cougar. Make sure that maps, gate keys, radios, and any other necessary logistical information are available to the capture team.

A complete wildlife attack report must be completed. The report may have a number of components, including: attack summary, site inspection, victim evidence, animal evidence, animal necropsy report and laboratory report.

11. Agencies should identify a single point of contact for media following human attacks.

For attack scenarios, lead agencies should designate an information officer to coordinate media contact. Ideally, the information officer should have a previously prepared response kit including: cellular phone with extra batteries and charger, notebook, camera, portable computer with printer, pager, paper, notepad, portable tape recorder, department phone roster, flashlight, media sign in sheets, clipboard, video camera, AM/FM radio, large markers, pens and so on. The information officer should be at the command post and easily accessible to media. Private individuals and other agency personnel involved with public safety animal incidents should be briefed about the role of the information officer in informing media. Do not allow employees to express their opinion, speculation, or hearsay to the media or general public about circumstances surrounding the incident or subsequent pursuit and capture of a cougar. Let the field team make the decisions about getting the correct animal. The media will probably attempt to photograph the cougar carcass. Agencies should discuss treating the carcass in a respectful manner, which may not be consistent with allowing it to be photographed.

Information the media will want:
- What happened?
- When?
- Was anyone injured or killed?
- Condition of surviving victim (this should be released only by the hospital or family)
- What is agency(s) doing?
- How long will it take?
- Who is responding?
- Is the public at risk? Why?
- Access to photographic opportunities
- Reports and other written documentation of the incident

If agency employees are interviewed independent of the information officer, they should:
- Never speculate about why something happened
- Never judge the site activities
- Never blame anyone for something happening
- Never try to be funny
- Never be late to the presentation
- Be honest—either you know or don't know the answer, or can or cannot answer, a question
- When you are uncertain, refer media person to Information Officer.

They should avoid:
- Pointing with fingers and shouting
- Interrupting others
- Dominating the interview
- Saying, "I'm glad that you asked"
- Answering too quickly
- Smiling or shaking head
- Wearing large flashy tie clasps, jewelry, photo sensitive glasses and sunglasses, etc.

CHAPTER 8

COUGAR RESEARCH AND MANAGEMENT INFORMATION

To promote sound research, we recommend the following:

1. Prioritize cougar research needs.

Cougar research carried out or supported by management agencies should provide reliable information for the adaptive management process. We partitioned research needs into 3 categories: 1) Priority research needs for wildlife managers to design and evaluate management actions; 2) Long-term research needs (i.e., 10-plus years) that benefit the management of cougars, other large mammals, and the landscapes they depend upon; and 3) Modeling needs that allow managers to structure hypotheses about management actions and environmental changes, and to conceptually inventory cougar populations.

PRIORITY RESEARCH NEEDS FOR ADAPTIVE MANAGEMENT

- Reliable maps of relative cougar density, habitat quality, and landscape linkages.
- Reliable, preferably non-invasive, methods to estimate or index cougar abundance.
- Investigate methods to assess cougar refuge areas relative to the zone managment concept.
- Effects of sport hunting harvest on cougar populations.
- Investigate the ability of source populations to restore sink populations.
- Effects of control actions on cougar populations and the management objective(s) the control actions are intended to influence (e.g., changes in survival rates in a wild ungulate population, or changes in livestock losses).
- Cougar behavior in wild and human-developed habitats; variation in cougar behavior around people and human developments.
- Effects of aversive conditioning on cougars.
- Human attitudes and values related to cougars.

Long-term Research

- Cougar population dynamics and natural history.
- Cougar habitat use patterns, use of habitat linkages, exploration movements, and responses to habitat changes.
- Relationships of cougars to prey populations.
- Relationships of cougars to other carnivores.
- Effectiveness of information and education programs about cougars on cougar management.

Model Development Needs

- Develop and validate models on cougar population dynamics.
- Develop and validate models for cougar habitat use.
- Develop and validate models on effects of cougar predation on prey populations.

2. Structure research according to the scientific method.

Research results would likely be reliable and accepted by professionals and the public if it followed 7 steps in rigorous scientific research outlined by Ratti and Garton (1996). After briefly listing each step, we provide a semi-hypothetical example related to cougar predation on bighorn sheep.

Research Question - Research questions should be clearly articulated. A thorough literature review should be conducted to survey information already existing on proposed research subjects. If there is little or no scientific information already available, then exploratory pilot studies and descriptive research phases need to be implemented to begin to gather objective, quantitative information on the problem. Once a body of information has accumulated on the problem, the next phase of research involves developing hypotheses.

Example: Cougar predation has been identified as a major limiting factor on some small populations of bighorn sheep (Wehausen 1996, Hayes et al. 2000, Schaefer et al. 2000, Logan and Sweanor 2001, Sawyer and Lindzey 2002). Let's assume a set of pilot studies over 3 years demonstrated that cougar predation was the main cause of mortality in 3 bighorn sheep populations of management concern. This leads to the question: Does removal of cougars cause bighorn survival rates to increase and enable bighorn populations to grow?

Hypothesis formulation - From results of descriptive research or extant theory on the problem, conceptual models or hypotheses should be devised that may explain natural phenomena or problems related to cougar management.

The hypotheses should include sets of predictions that should be supported if the hypotheses are credible explanations for phenomena.

Example: There is limited field evidence demonstrating that removal of cougars that kill bighorn sheep substantially reduces cougar predation rates (Logan and Sweanor 2001:350-354). Ross et al. (1997) showed that an individual cougar can cause substantial predation on a bighorn sheep population, and that removal of such an individual slowed the rate of sheep population decline. Furthermore, Ernest et al. (2002) used a model to show that fewer cougars would need to be removed through targeted removals (of cougars known to kill or associated with bighorn sheep) rather than nonselective removals to achieve the same level of benefit for a bighorn population. This suggests hypothesis H1: Removal of individual cougars that kill bighorn sheep cause the sheep population to increase. An alternate hypothesis might be H2: Nonselective removals of cougars cause the sheep population to increase. Ideally, another area would be available where no cougars would be removed, and the working hypothesis or prediction would be that the sheep population would decline in this area.

Hypothesis testing and research design - Experimental research should be designed to test each hypothesis whenever possible. The credibility of any particular hypothesis increases as attendant predictions are supported and as alternate hypotheses and their predictions are rejected. Research designs should always consider how the data will be treated statistically. Statisticians should be part of the planning process to ensure appropriate sample sizes and data gathering and data analyses methods.

Example: These hypotheses can be tested experimentally in the adaptive management process in various ways. Researchers in several states might choose study areas where bighorn sheep populations are a concern, and randomly allocate these to treatment (targeted removal of sheep-killing cougars, nonselective removal of cougars) and control areas. Cougar and bighorn sheep population dynamics will be monitored in each area for 3 years before treatment and 3 years after treatment, followed by crossover of treatment and control designations. The focus of the research would be variation in cougar predation rates and agent-specific mortality rates in sheep, and sheep population dynamics in relation to cougar removal and changes in the cougar population.

Unreplicated case study can also provide meaningful insights into predator-prey relationships, especially in a Before-After-Control-Impact (BACI) study design (Stewart-Oaten and Murdoch 1986, Stewart-Oaten and Bence 2001). Underwood (1992, 1994) suggests that using one impacted, and several control, locations can more reliably detect effects, including those that do not affect long-run mean abundances, but do alter temporal variance.

Data collection - Experienced personnel and political, administrative, and financial support must be committed to the research effort to ensure it is properly carried through to completion. Personnel responsible for project design, data analyses, and interpretations should be directly involved in the field research so that they are genuinely knowledgeable about the data gathering process, field logistics, capabilities of personnel and equipment, the natural history of study animals, and the environment in which the study is conducted.

Example: This field-intensive experimental research would require highly motivated field ecologists experienced in cougar and bighorn sheep ecology. The project would also be expensive and require the removal of cougars, which might not be acceptable to some segments of the public. Therefore, commitment by supporting management agencies would need to be strong and consistent over the duration of the project.

Evaluation and interpretation - Analyses and presentation of data, reporting of descriptive and experimental research, and the testing of hypotheses should be clear and concise. Murtaugh (2002) argues that BACI studies should rely on graphical presentation, expert judgment, and common sense, rather than P values associated with hypothesis tests. Principal attention should be to effect sizes. There should be a synthesis that best explains the biological phenomena associated with the research problem given the data. The goal of the research should be to impart reliable knowledge that will aid managers to adapt cougar management to the new state of knowledge and management needs, and to address concerns of public stakeholders.

Example: Researchers find that removal of individual offending cougars effectively caused sheep population increase, and the rate of increase was greater than in the nonselective removal and control areas. In the adaptive management process, this becomes the preferred method of managing cougars where sheep populations of concern might be limited mainly by cougar predation.

Speculation and new hypotheses - Research that is well designed and carried out by attentive researchers should spawn additional questions and speculation that could be structured into additional hypotheses that may be investigated in future research.

Example: In one bighorn population, cougar removal did not result in sheep population increase, because as cougars were removed a greater proportion of sheep died from pneumonia (i.e., cougar predation deaths were compensatory). Then researchers might hypothesize H3: Pneumonia is the main factor limiting the sheep population.

Publication - The research effort should be written in the format of an article for submission to peer-reviewed journals or as a peer-reviewed book so that the information is available to other wildlife professionals. The information should also be formatted so it can be published in popular articles for interested lay stakeholders.

3. Validate and justify population models.

Population models may help managers anticipate potential effects of management strategies (e.g., changes in harvest rates) before they are actually implemented. Habitat models may help managers to reliably identify cougar habitat and potential landscape linkages over huge areas. Models of cougar-prey interactions may help managers to understand the potential impacts of cougar predation on ungulate populations of special concern. Population and cougar-prey models might also be used retrospectively to help managers understand what might have happened to animal populations given a set of assumptions and data. When models are developed, we urge that models be tested with real data. For example, a cougar population model might be tested by comparing model outputs with parameter estimates from intensively studied cougar populations to see if model output is consistent with dynamics of real cougar populations.

Model users should never assume that the model is the population or the real world situation. Models are tools that are sometimes useful for helping managers to understand natural phenomena. In addition, when models are used, users should list all assumptions and biologically and theoretically justify all parameters so that other users can understand the structure and utility of such models. In addition, sensitivity analyses should be conducted to help managers understand influential parameters and how to structure data gathering processes (also see Chapter 4: Assessing Cougar Populations).

4. Be realistic and collaborate in cougar research.

In designing research, it is important to realistically consider the natural history of cougars—animals that are cryptic, difficult to capture, occur at low densities, and are long-lived. Study area sizes required for cougar population level studies will place constraints on where such research can be conducted because of other user interests of the landscape, including ranching, hunting, and energy and urban developments. Sometimes study area choice will be focused on a particular area because of management-oriented problems—for example, high cougar predation rates on an endangered bighorn sheep population, or a focal area of cougar-human conflict. Therefore, choice of study area locations and the attendant cougar population will not be random.

Furthermore, there may not be enough resources (i.e., funding, personnel, or equipment) or habitat available to have replicates of treatment or control areas on similar cougar habitats. As such, different wildlife agencies from different states should consider collaborating in long-term experimental research projects to provide adequate funding and treatment, control, and replicate research areas. Studies involving cougar population dynamics or relationships of cougars to other mammals will need to be at least 10 years in duration. It should be recognized that environmental conditions may change during the study (e.g., wet or drought periods, fire) that may confound results from certain experimental manipulations, but they will also provide information on temporal variation.

Recognize that no one researcher can be an expert at everything. Therefore, when research programs are multi-faceted, develop a collaborative group of experts who specialize in different fields. For example, a research project aimed at developing and testing DNA genotype mark-recapture methods to estimate cougar numbers will probably provide the most reliable information about such methods if carried out by a group comprised of field biologists trained to appropriately sample the cougar population, geneticists to genotype individual cougars and estimate genotype error rates, experts in mark-recapture modeling to help choose the most appropriate models and estimates, and biometricians to assist in project design and data analysis.

5. Standardize reporting methods.

The difficulty, cost, and politics of cougar research projects will continue to constrain the number, distribution, and conduct of such projects. Therefore, sample size (i.e., number of projects in a variety of environmental and experimental settings) will accumulate only with the accumulation of research findings from different parts of the cougar range over time. Thus, researchers should carefully report their study methods and the research environment so that wildlife managers and other researchers can distinguish real similarities and differences among cougar populations under study.

For example, cougar density is one of the most important parameters used by managers to conceptually inventory cougar populations and estimate harvest rates. Generally, when direct information about cougar density in a particular

region or state does not exist, managers choose from a range of cougar densities reported in the literature and then extrapolate them to what they subjec-
tively deem to be "similar environments." Also, researchers sometimes synthesize cougar densities gathered by a number of research projects. Yet, little
consideration is given to the reliability of those parameter estimates, partially
because the research and reporting methods are not adequately described in
the literature. The basic assumption is that the variation in population density
estimates is real. However, much of the inter-population variation may be due
to unequal research efforts.

Using cougar density estimates as an example, here is how information in
published reports could be standardized to facilitate meaningful interpretations and comparisons. Reports should include: 1) how the study area was
chosen; 2) maps of the study area and its spatial location within a broader
region; 3) information on cougar management and human impacts before and
during the research; 4) how study area boundaries were chosen; 5) geo-physical
and biological characteristics of the study area; 6) a description of the sampling
methods; 7) amount of research effort expended to capture and mark cougars

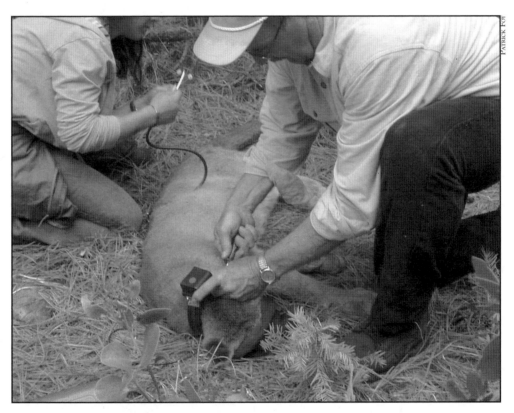

*Safe, effective protocols for the live capture of cougars are needed for the protection of cougars and research
personnel.*

and to search for unmarked cougars (e.g., total number of days searching for cougar per year or season, trap days per year, number of days per capture); 8) number of cougars captured, marked, and released; 9) how the cougar population was estimated; and 10) how cougar density was estimated.

We urge researchers to structure ways of standardizing reporting methods whenever feasible during the literature review phase at the beginning of the planning process. Such standards should apply to all aspects of cougar biology and ecology.

6. Follow safe capture, handling, and euthanasia protocols when researching and managing cougars.

Many capture methods involve considerable risk for cougars and research personnel. Safe, effective protocols for the live capture of cougars of various ages can be found in the following references: Logan et al. 1986, Logan et al. 1999, Kreeger et al. 2002. Guidelines for safe euthanasia of cougars are in Kreeger et al. (2002).

ABOUT THE AUTHORS

TOM BECK

Tom spent 25 years as a carnivore research biologist with the Colorado Division of Wildlife. His field research included natural history studies of black bears, the physiology of bear hibernation, river otter reintroduction in desert rivers, and kit fox inventory and recovery. He also served as principle author analyst on statewide management plans for black bears, cougars, river otters, coyotes and furbearers as well as working on multi-agency teams for lynx introduction and swift fox conservation. His published work spans a range of topics from bear physiology to ethical consideration of hunting management. He is now retired and living in Colorado.

JOHN BEECHAM

John worked for the Idaho Department of Fish and Game for over 29 years. He spent 12 years studying black bears in Idaho and the last 15 years in the headquarters office in Boise, where he supervised the wildlife research program and the black bear and cougar management programs.

He has spent the majority of his career working on bears. He has published numerous papers on bears and coauthored, with Jeff Rohlman, a book entitled *A Shadow in the Forest - Idaho's Black Bear* that was published by the University of Idaho Press in 1994. John is currently affiliated with Beringia South's large carnivore program, and has been working on a variety of national and international bear and cougar projects since his retirement in 1999.

PAUL BEIER

Paul is professor of Conservation Biology and Wildlife Ecology in the School of Forestry at Northern Arizona University. His 1988-1992 study of cougars is best known for its documentation that dispersing cougars use habitat corridors in urban southern California. Since then he has worked on "missing linkages" efforts in California, Arizona, and elsewhere, to promote collaborative, science-based efforts to maintain landscape connectivity on ecoregional scales. He has also studied Mexican spotted owls, northern goshawks, and forest bird communities in the United States and West Africa.

In 2003, he coauthored a massive review of scientific literature on the Florida panther. He works with traditional chiefs in West Africa to create and manage community-based wildlife sanctuaries, serves on the Board of Governors of the Society for Conservation Biology, and is an active member of The Wildlife Society.

TERRY HOFSTRA

Terry is currently chief of Resource Management and Science at Redwood National and State Parks, where he has been involved in a wide variety of fish and wildlife research and management projects and where he currently manages a major land rehabilitation program. In 1994 he organized a workshop of scientists and managers to begin development of management strategies for dealing with the increasing number of cougar-human incidents in parks. A recipient of the *National Park Service Director's Award for Natural Resource Management*, Terry has also worked for the National Park Service's Denver Service Center and the Environmental Protection Agency.

MAURICE HORNOCKER

Maurice began his work with cougars in 1964 in the central Idaho wilderness. Since that time he and his students and colleagues have studied cougar populations in several other regions in the western United States. He has also studied other big cat species around the world. He served as leader of the Idaho Cooperative Wildlife Research Unit at the University of Idaho from 1968 to 1985. In 1985 he founded the Hornocker Wildlife Institute and served as its director until 2000 when the Institute merged with the Wildlife Conservation Society. He currently is a senior conservationist with WCS and lives in Bellevue, Idaho.

FRED LINDZEY

Fred is an emeritus professor at the University of Wyoming. He recently retired from the Department of Interior's Cooperative Research Unit program after 20 years. He previously served as a faculy member at Utah State University and the University of New Hampshire. Fred and his students have worked on cougar management questions in Utah, Wyoming and Colorado. He has also worked with other carnivores including coyotes, swift foxes, jaguars, ocelots, black and grizzly bears, and badgers. Other research interests include the affect of gas and oil development on western ungulates.

KENNETH LOGAN

Ken is a field biologist who has been studying cougars since 1981. He has also studied mule deer, bighorn sheep, and elk. His cougar research has been conducted in Wyoming, New Mexico, and California. During his efforts, Ken has been employed by the University of Wyoming, the Hornocker Wildlife Institute, and the University of California at Davis. Currently he is the carnivore researcher for the Colorado Division of Wildlife and is studying cougar ecology on the Uncompahgre Plateau.

He has published numerous peer-reviewed scientific writings on cougars, including a book he co-authored with Linda Sweanor, entitled, *Desert Puma: Evolutionary Ecology and Conservation of an Enduring Carnivore*, which was awarded *The Outstanding Publication in Wildlife Ecology and Management* by The Wildlife Society in 2002.

BECKY PIERCE

Becky is an associate wildlife biologist with the California Department of Fish and Game. Becky has been studying cougars in the eastern Sierra Nevada since 1991 and currently is the predator specialist for the Department's Sierra Nevada Bighorn Sheep Recovery Program. Her past research focused on predator-prey interactions of cougars and mule deer, and the population biology and behavior of cougars. Since then she has focused on the interaction of cougars with the endangered Sierra Nevada bighorn sheep to assist in their recovery. Becky is an affiliate professor with the University of Alaska, Fairbanks; an affiliate faculty member at Idaho State University; a research associate with the Institute of Arctic Biology; and advises several graduate students. She also is an associate editor for *Western North American Naturalist*, and publishes regularly in the peer-reviewed literature.

HOWARD QUIGLEY

Howard obtained his PhD from the University of Idaho in 1988 and subsequently joined the faculty in the University of Maryland system before returning to Idaho, where he has served as president of the Hornocker Wildlife Institute for nearly eight years. From 2000 to 2002, he was director of the Global Carnivore Program at the Wildlife Conservation Society, and currently serves as executive director of Beringia South, a non-profit science and education organization in Kelly, Wyoming. Howard has been involved in nearly two dozen cougar field projects in the western United States and Latin America, as well as field projects on jaguars, Asiatic leopards, and Siberian tigers. He is the author of more than 30 professional papers.

IAN ROSS

Ian was an original member of the Cougar Management Guidelines Working Group until his death in 2003. He graduated from the University of Guelph with an honors degree in wildlife biology in 1982. He began his field career working on a variety of wildlife species including snapping turtles and black bears. From the early 1980s until his death Ian worked on cougars in southwest Alberta and helped draft the cougar management plan for Alberta and a conservation strategy for large carnivores in Canada. He also spent many years studying grizzly bears. Ian was the senior author of nine papers in peer-reviewed journals in addition to many other technical reports. While studying African lions, Ian was killed in a plane crash. As he wished, Ian was cremated and his ashes dispersed in Kananaskis Country, a place where had spent a lot of time with his cougars.

HARLEY SHAW

Harley grew up in Arizona and started working for the Arizona Game and Fish Department in 1955. He has been involved in wildlife management for 48 years, of which 27 years were as a research biologist studying mule deer, wild turkey, bighorn, and cougar. He organized and hosted the Third Mountain Lion Workshop in Prescott, Arizona. He retired from the Arizona Game and Fish Department in 1990 but continued to write, consult, and work with citizen groups on wildlife monitoring.

He has published two books: *Soul Among Lions* and *Stalking the Big Bird*, both through University of Arizona Press. He also published the *Mountain Lion Field Guide*, which has undergone multiple printings. He now resides in Hillsboro, New Mexico.

ROLLIN SPARROWE

Rollin has more than 35 years' experience with state and federal wildlife management in North America. During his 22 years with the United States Fish and Wildlife Service, he blended science with policy on a variety of topics, including the harvest of migratory birds. Rollin recently retired from serving as the president of the Wildlife Management Institute, a position he held from 1991 to 2004.

Rollin received the *Meritorious Service Award* from the Department of Interior in 1991. In 2002, he received the *Aldo Leopold Memorial Award* from The Wildlife Society for his 35-year record of distinguished federal and non-governmental service to wildlife conservation. Rollin is an avid hunter and fisherman, and lives in Daniel, Wyoming.

STEVE TORRES

Steve has been studying large mammals since 1981. He is currently a staff environmental scientist with the California Department of Fish and Game, Resource Assessment Program. From 1992 to 2002, Steve was the state's lead for bighorn sheep and mountain lion management. He continues to be active in mountain lion research and his interest focuses on modeling habitat suitability, conservation planning, and understanding the factors influencing mountain lion and human conflicts.

To address the growing interest and questions surrounding mountain lions, he published a book in 1997 entitled *Mountain Lion Alert*. This book is now being updated and re-published as *Lion Sense*. Steve has written numerous scientific and magazine articles on cougars and bighorn sheep.

SHARON NEGRI, *Project Director*

Sharon has over 25 years of experience working on wildlife policy and conservation projects. She has worked in various state and local agencies addressing transportation, water, and marine issues. Sharon founded WildFutures in 1994 to help bridge the gap between the scientific and the conservation communities for the protection of wildlife and their habitats, with a special emphasis on carnivores. Since 1994, WildFutures has met high priority needs through a combination of networking, research and education. Sharon works to bring diverse groups and scientists together to develop innovative strategies to solve wildlife issues.

As project director for the Cougar Management Guidelines Working Group, Sharon coordinated logistics, arranged meetings, raised funds, and managed the process of publishing the Cougar Management Guidelines.

LITERATURE CITED

Ackerman, B. B., F. G. Lindzey, and T. P. Hemker. 1984. Cougar food habits in southern Utah. Journal of Wildlife Management 48:147-155.

Ackerman, B. B., F. G. Lindzey, and T. P. Hemker. 1986. Predictive energetics model for cougars. Pages 333-352 in S. D. Miller and D. Everett, editors. Cats of the World: Biology, Conservation, and Management. National Wildlife Federation, Washington D.C., USA.

Albon, S. D., T. N. Coulson, D. Brown, F. E. Guinness, J. M. Pemberton, and T. H. Clutton-Brock. 2000. Temporal changes in key factors and key age groups influencing the population dynamics of female red deer. Journal of Animal Ecology 69:1099-1110.

Andelt, W. F. 1999. Relative effectiveness of guarding-dog breeds to deter predation on domestic sheep in Colorado. Wildlife Society Bulletin 27:706-714.

Anderson, A. E. 1981. Morphological and physiological characteristics. Pages 27-97 in O. C. Wallmo, editors. Mule and Black-tailed Deer of North America. University of Nebraska Press, Lincoln, Nebraska, USA.

_____. 1983. A critical review of literature on puma (Felis concolor). Special Report No. 54. Colorado Division of Wildlife, Fort Collins, Colorado, USA.

_____, D. C. Bowden, and D. M. Kattner. 1992. The puma on Uncompahgre Plateau, Colorado. Colorado Division of Wildlife Technical Publication 40, Fort Collins, Colorado, USA.

Anderson, C. R. Jr. 2003. Cougar ecology, management and population genetics in Wyoming. Dissertation, University of Wyoming, Laramie, Wyoming, USA.

_____, and F. G. Lindzey. 2000. Estimating sex reporting bias in mountain lions using DNA analysis. 6th Mountain Lion Workshop, San Antonio.

_____, _____. 2003. Estimating cougar predation rates from GPS location clusters. Journal of Wildlife Management 67:307-316.

_____, _____. In press. Experimental evaluation of populations trend and harvest composition in a Wyoming cougar population. Wildlife Society Bulletin.

_____, _____, and D. B. McDonald. 2004. Genetic structure of cougar populations across the Wyoming Basin: metapopulation or megapopulation. Journal of Mammalogy 85 (6). In press.

Ashman, D., G. C. Christensen, M. L. Hess, G. K. Tsukamoto, and M. S. Wickersham. 1983. The mountain lion in Nevada. Nevada Game and Fish Department, unpublished report Pittman-Robertson Project W-48-15.

Aune, K. E. 1991. Increasing mountain lion populations and human-mountain lion interactions in Montana. Pages 86-94 *in* C. E. Braun, editor. Mountain Lion-Human Interactions: Symposium and Workshop. Colorado Division of Wildlife, Denver, Colorado, USA.

Bailey, J. A. 1984. Principles of Wildlife Management. John Wiley & Sons, New York, New York, USA.

Ballard, W. B., L. A. Ayres, P. R. Krausman, D. J. Reed, and S. G. Fancy. 1997. Ecology of wolves in relation to a migratory caribou herd in northwest Alaska. Wildlife Monographs 135:1-47.

Barnhurst, D. 1986. Vulnerability of cougars to hunting. Thesis, Utah State University, Logan, Utah, USA.

_____, and F. G. Lindzey. 1989. Detecting female mountain lions with kittens. Northwest Science 63:35-37.

Bartmann, R. M., G. C. White, and L. H. Carpenter. 1992. Compensatory mortality in a Colorado mule deer population. Wildlife Monographs 121:1-39.

Bauer, J. W., K. A. Logan, L. L. Sweanor, and W. M. Boyce. Submitted. Scavenging behavior in puma. The Southwestern Naturalist.

Becker, E. F. 1991. A terrestrial furbearer estimator based on probability sampling. Journal of Wildlife Management 55:730-737.

Beier, P. 1991. Cougar attacks on humans in the United States and Canada. Wildlife Society Bulletin 19:403-412.

_____. 1993. Determining minimum habitat areas and habitat corridors for cougars. Conservation Biology 7:94-108.

_____. 1995. Dispersal of juvenile cougars in fragmented habitat. Journal of Wildlife Management 59:228-237.

_____. 1996. Metapopulation modeling, tenacious tracking, and cougar conservation. Pages 293-323 *in* D. R. McCullough, editor. Metapopulations and Wildlife Management. Island Press, Washington D.C., USA.

_____, and R. F. Noss. 1998. Do habitat corridors provide connectivity? Conservation Biology 12:1241-1252.

_____, and R. H. Barrett. 1993. The cougar in the Santa Ana Mountain Range California. Final Report to California Department of Fish and Game.

_____, and S. C. Cunningham. 1996. Power of track surveys to detect changes in cougar populations. Wildlife Society Bulletin 24:540-546.

_____, and S. Loe. 1992. A checklist for evaluating impacts to wildlife movement corridors. Wildlife Society Bulletin 20:434-440.

_____, D. Choate, and R. H. Barrett. 1995. Movement patterns of mountain lions during different behaviors. Journal of Mammalogy 76:1056-1070.

_____, K. Penrod, C. Luke, W. D. Spencer, and C. Cabañero. 2005. South Coast Missing Linkages: restoring connectivity to wildlands in the largest metropolitan area in the United States. Invited Chapter *in* K. Crooks and M. A. Sanjayan, editors. Connectivity and Conservation, Oxford University Press (pending).

_____, M. R. Vaughan, M. J. Conroy, and H. Quigley. 2003. An analysis of scientific literature related to the Florida panther. Florida Fish and Wildlife Conservation Commission Special Report.

Beissinger, S. R., and M. I. Westphal. 1998. On the use of demographic models of population viability in endangered species management. Journal of Wildlife Management 62:821-841.

Bergerud, A. T., W. Wyett, and J. B. Snider. 1983. The role of wolf predation in limiting a moose population. Journal of Wildlife Management 47:977-988.

Bleich, V. C., and T. J. Taylor. 1998. Survivorship and cause-specific mortality in five populations of mule deer. The Great Basin Naturalist 58:265-272.

Bonenfant, C., J. M. Gaillard, F. Klein, and A. Loison. 2002. Sex- and age-dependent effects of population density on life history traits of red deer _Cervus elaphus_ in a temperate forest. Ecography 25:446-458.

Bowyer, R. T., D. K. Person, and B. M. Pierce. 2005. Detecting top-down verses bottom–up regulation of ungulates by large carnivores: implications for conservation of biodiversity _in_ J. C. Ray, K. H. Redford, R. S. Steneck, and J. Berger, editors. Large Carnivores and the Conservation of Biodiversity. Island Press, Washington D.C., USA.

_____, M. C. Nicholson, E. M. Molvar, and J. B. Faro. 1999. Moose on Kalgin Island: are density-dependent processes related to harvest? Alces 35:73-89.

_____, V. Van Ballenberge, and J. G. Kie. 1997. The role of moose in landscape processes: effects of biogeography, population dynamics, and predation. Pages 265-287 _in_ J. S. Bissonette, editor. Wildlife and Landscape Ecology: Effects and Patterns of Scale. Springer-Verlag, New York, New York, USA.

Boyce, M. S. 1989. The Jackson elk herd: intensive wildlife management in North America. Cambridge University Press, New York, New York, USA.

Boyd, D. K., and G. K. Neale. 1992. An adult cougar, _Felis concolor_, killed by gray wolves, _Canis lupus_, in Glacier National Park, Montana. Canadian Field Naturalist 106:524-525.

Caughley, G. 1977. Analysis of vertebrate populations. Wiley, New York, New York, USA.

_____. 1979. What is this thing called carrying capacity? Pages 2-8 _in_ M. S. Boyce and L. D. Hayden-Wing, editors. North American Elk: Ecology, Behavior, and Management. University of Wyoming, Laramie, Wyoming, USA.

Charnov, E. L. 2001. Evolution of mammal life histories. Evolutionary Ecology Research 3:521-535.

Christensen, G. C., and R. J. Fischer. 1976. Transactions of the Mountain Lion Workshop. U. S. Fish and Wildlife Service and Nevada Fish and Game Department. Sparks, Nevada, USA.

Clutton-Brock, T. H., A. W. Illius, K. Wilson, B. T. Grenfell, A. D. C. MacColl, and S. D. Albon. 1997. Stability and instability in ungulate populations: an empirical analysis. American Naturalist 149:195-219.

Connolly, E. J. Jr. 1949. Food habits and life history of the mountain lion (*Felis concolor hippolestes*). Thesis, University of Utah, Salt Lake City, Utah, USA.

Craig, D. L. 1986. The seasonal food habits in sympatric populations of puma (*Puma concolor*), coyote (*Canis latrans*), and bobcat (*Lynx rufus*) in the Diablo Range of California. Thesis, San Jose State University, San Jose, California, USA.

Cramer, P. C. and K. M. Portier. 2001. Modeling Florida panther movements in response to human attributes of the landscape and ecological settings. Ecological Modeling 140:51-80.

Culver, M., W. E. Johnson, J. Pecon-Slattery, and S. J. O'Brien. 2000. Genomic ancestry of the American puma (*Puma concolor*). Journal of Heredity 91:186-197.

Cunningham, S. C., L. A. Haynes, C. Gustavson and D. D. Haywood. 1995. Evaluation of the interaction between mountain lions and cattle in the Aravaipa-Klondyke area of southeast Arizona. Arizona Game and Fish Department Technical Report 17.

Dawn, D. 2002. Cougar management in the Western United States: an analysis of hunting harvest strategies. Thesis, San Jose State University, San Jose, California, USA.

DeSimone, R., B. Semmens, B. Shinn, T. Chilton, J. Sikich, and B. Weisner. 2002. Garnet Mountains mountain lion research. Progress Report January 2001-December 2002. Montana Fish Wildlife and Parks, Helena, Montana, USA.

Dickson, B. G., J. S. Jenness, and P. Beier. 2005. Influence of vegetation, roads, and topography on cougar movement in southern California. Journal of Wildlife Management 69:264-276.

Dunbar, M. R., R. Velarde, M. A. Gregg, and M. Bray. 1999. Health evaluation of a pronghorn antelope population in Oregon. Journal of Wildlife Diseases 35:496-510.

Eberhardt, L. L. 1977. Optimal policies for conservation of large mammals, with special reference to marine ecosystems. Environmental Conservation 4:205-212.

Ellingson, J. 2003. Mountain lion activity and movement patterns relative to human activities in the Redwood Creek Basin of northwest California. Thesis, University of Idaho, Moscow, Idaho, USA.

Ernest, H. B., E. S. Rubin, and W. M. Boyce. 2002. Fecal DNA analysis and risk assessment of mountain lion predation of bighorn sheep. Journal of Wildlife Management 66:75-85.

_____, W. M. Boyce, V. C. Bleich, B. May, S. J. Stiver, and S. G. Torres. 2003. Genetic structure of mountain lion (*Puma concolor*) populations in California. Conservation Genetics 4:353-366.

Eve, J. H., and F. E. Kellogg. 1977. Management implications of abosomal parasites in southeastern white-tailed deer. Journal of Wildlife Management 41:169-177.

Fithzugh, E. L. 1988. Managing with potential for cougar attacks against humans. Pages 74-76 *in* R. H. Smith, editor. Proceedings Third Cougar Workshop, The Wildlife Society, and Arizona Game and Fish Department, Phoenix, Arizona, USA.

_____, M. W. Kenyon, and K. Etling. 2003. Lessening the impact of a cougar attack on a human *in* Proceedings of the Seventh Cougar Workshop, Jackson, Wyoming, USA.

Forchhammer, M. C., T. H. Clutton-Brock, J. Lindstroem, and S. D. Albon. 2001. Climate and population density induce long-term cohort variation in a northern ungulate. Journal of Animal Ecology 70:721-729.

Fowler, C. W. 1981. Density dependence as related to life history strategy. Ecology 62:602-610.

French, C. E., L. C. McEwen, N. D. Magruder, R. N. Ingram, and R. W. Swift. 1956. Nutrient requirements for growth and antler development in white-tailed deer. Journal of Wildlife Management 20:221-232.

Gasaway, W. C., R. D. Boertje, D. V. Grangaard, D. G. Kelleyhouse, R. O. Stephenson, and D. G. Larsen. 1992. The role of predation in limiting moose at low densities in Alaska and Yukon and implications for conservation. Wildlife Monographs 120:1-59.

Gigliotti, L. M., D. Fecske, and J. Jenks. 2002. Mountain lions in South Dakota: a public opinion survey-2002. South Dakota State University, Brookings and South Dakota Game, Fish and Parks, Pierre, South Dakota, USA.

Gould, W. R., and J. D. Nichols. 1998. Estimation of temporal variability of survival in animal populations. Ecology 79:2531–2538.

Haber, G. C. 1977. Socio-ecological dynamics of wolves and prey in a subarctic ecosystem. Dissertation. University British Columbia, Vancouver, British Columbia, Canada.

Halfpenny, J. C., M. R. Sanders, and K. A. McGrath. 1991. Human-cougar interactions in Boulder County, Colorado: past, present, and future. Pages 86-94 *in* C. S. Braun, editor. Cougar-Human Interaction Symposium and Workshop. Colorado Division of Wildlife, Denver, Colorado, USA.

Hansen, K. 1992. Cougar, the American lion. Northland Publishing, Flagstaff, Arizona, USA.

Harlow, H. J., F. G. Lindzey, and W. A. Gern. 1992. Stress response of cougars to nonlethal pursuit by hunters. Canadian Journal of Zoology 70:136-139.

Harrison, R. L. 1992. Toward a theory of inter-refuge corridor design. Conservation Biology 6:292-25.

Harrison, S. 1990. Cougar predation on bighorn sheep in the Junction Wildlife Management Area, British Columbia. Thesis, University of British Columbia, Vancouver, Canada.

Hayes, C. J., E. S. Rubin, M. C. Jorgensen, R. A. Botta, and W. M. Boyce. 2000. Mountain lion predation of bighorn sheep in the peninsular ranges, California. Journal of Wildlife Management 64:954-959.

Hemker T. P., F. G. Lindzey, and B. B. Ackerman 1984. Population characteristics and movement patterns of cougars in southern Utah. Journal of Wildlife Management 48:1275-1284.

_____, _____, _____, and A. J. Button. 1982. Survival of cougar cubs in a non-hunted population. Pages 327-332 in S. D. Miller, and D. D. Everett, editors. Proceeding of the International Cat Symposium, Kingsville, Texas, USA.

Holm, G. W. 2003. What does ten years (1993-2002) of mountain lion observation data reveal about mountain lion-human interactions within Redwood National and State Parks? Abstract in Proceedings of the Seventh Cougar Workshop, Jackson, Wyoming, USA.

Hofstra, T. 1995a. Draft cougar guidelines. Unpublished file report. Redwood National Park, Orick, California, USA.

_____. 1995b. Track of the cat. Ranger: The Journal of the Association of National Park Rangers. Summer 1995, 20-21.

Holling, C. S. 1959. The components of predation as revealed by a study of small mammal predation of the European pine sawfly. Canadian Entomologist 91:293-320.

Hopkins, R. A., M. J. Kutilek, and G. L. Shreve. 1986. The density and home range characteristics of cougars in the Diablo Range of California. Pages 223-235, in S. D. Miller and D. D. Everett, editors. Cats of the world: Biology, Conservation and Management. National Wildlife Federation, Washington, D. C., USA.

Hopkins, R. A. 1989. Ecology of the Puma in the Diablo Range. Dissertation, University of California Berkeley, California, USA.

Hornocker, M. G. 1970. An analysis of mountain lion predation upon mule deer and elk in the Idaho primitive area. Wildlife Monograph 21:1-39.

Hutchinson, G. E. 1957. Concluding remarks. Population Studies: Animal Ecology and Demography. Cold Spring Harbor Symposia on Quantitative Biology 22:415-427.

Iriarte, J. A., W. L. Franklin, W. E. Johnson, and K. H. Redford. 1990. Biogeographic variation of food habits and body size of the America puma. Oecologia 85:185-190

Jordan, P. A., B. E. McLaren, and S. M. Sell. 2000. A summary of research on moose and related ecological topics at Isle Royale, USA. Alces 36:233-267.

Jorgenson, J. T. , M. Festa-Bianchet, J. M. Gaillard, and W. D. Wishart. 1997. Effects of age, sex disease, and density on survival of bighorn sheep. Ecology 78:1019-1032.

Kamler, J. F., R. M. Lee, J. C. deVos, Jr., W. B. Ballard, and H. A. Whitlaw. 2002. Survival and cougar predation of translocated bighorn sheep in Arizona. Journal of Wildlife Management 66:1267-1272.

Karanth, K. U. and J. D. Nichols. 2000. Ecological status and conservation of tigers in India. Final technical report to the Division of International Conservation, U.S. Fish and Wildlife Service, Washington, D. C., USA; Wildlife Conservation Society, New York, New York, USA; and Centre for Wildlife Studies, Banglore, India.

Keech, M. A., R. T. Bowyer, J. M. Ver Hoef, R. D. Boertje, B. W. Dale, and T. R. Stephenson. 2000. Life-history consequences of maternal condition in Alaskan moose. Journal of Wildlife Management 64:450-462.

Kellert, S. R. and C. P. Smith. 2001. Human values toward large mammals. Pages 30-63, *in* S. Demarias and P. Krausman, editors. Ecology and Management of Large Mammals in North America. Prentice Hall, Upper Saddle River, New Jersey, USA.

Kie, J. G., R. T. Bowyer, and K. M. Stewart. 2003. Ungulates in western forests: habitat requirements, population dynamics, and ecosystem processes. Pages 296-340 *in* C. Zabel, and R. Anthony, editors. Mammal Community Dynamics: Management and Conservation in the Coniferous Forest of Western North America. Cambridge University Press, New York, New York, USA.

Koehler G. M., and M. G. Hornocker. 1991. Seasonal resource use among mountain lions, bobcats, and coyotes. Journal of Mammalogy 72:391-396.

Krausman, P. R. and E. D. Ables. 1981. Ecology of the Carmen Mountains white-tailed deer. Scientific monograph series: 15. Washington, U.S. Department of the Interior, National Park Service.

Kreeger, T. J., J. M. Arnemo, and J. P. Raath. 2002. Handbook of Wildlife Chemical Immobilization: International Edition. Wildlife Pharmaceuticals, Incorporated, Ft. Collins, Colorado, USA.

Kunkel, K. E., T. K. Ruth, D. H. Pletscher, and M. G. Hornocker. 1999. Winter prey selection by wolves and cougars in and near Glacier National Park. Journal of Wildlife Management 63:901-910.

Laing, S. P., and F. G. Lindzey. 1991. Cougar habitat selection in south-central Utah. Pages 86-94 *in* C. S. Braun, editor. Cougar-Human Interaction Symposium and Workshop, Colorado Division of Wildlife, Denver, Colorado, USA.

Land, E. D., M. Lotz, D.B. Shindle, and S. K. Taylor. 1999. Florida panther genetic restoration and management. Annual Report 1998-99. Florida Fish and Wildlife Conservation Commission, Tallahassee, Florida, USA.

Laundré, J. W., and L. Hernandez. 2003. Winter hunting habitat of pumas Puma concolor in northwestern Utah and southern Idaho, USA. Wildlife Biology 9:123-129.

_____, and T. W. Clark. Managing puma hunting in the western United States through a metapopulation approach. 2003. Animal Conservation 6:159-170.

Leopold, A. S. 1933. Game Management. Scribners, New York.

_____, R. J. Gutierrez, and M. T. Bronson. 1981. North American Game Birds and Mammals. Charles Scribner's Sons, New York, New York USA.

Leyhausen, P. 1979. Cat behaviour: the predatory and social behaviour of domestic and wild cats. Translated by B. A. Tonkin. Garland Press, New York, New York, USA.

Lindzey, F. G. 1987. Mountain lion. Pages 656-668 *in* M. Novak, J. A. Baker, M. E. Obbard, and B. Malloch, editors. Wild Furbearer Management and Conservation in North America. Ontario Trappers Association and Ontario Ministry of Natural Resources, Toronto, Canada.

_____. 1991. Managing mountain lions in a changing social environment. Pages 181-182 *in* C. E. Braun, editor. Mountain Lion-Human Interactions. Colorado Division of Wildlife, Denver, Colorado, USA.

_____, B. B. Ackerman, D. Barnhurst, and T. P. Hemker. 1988. Survival rates of mountain lions in southern Utah. Journal of Wildlife Management 52:664-667.

_____, W. D. Vansickle, B. B. Ackerman, D. Barnhurst, T. P. Hemker, and S. P. Laing. 1994. Cougar population dynamics in southern Utah. Journal of Wildlife Management 58:619-624.

_____, W. D. VanSickle, S. P. Laing, and C. S. Mecham. 1992. Cougar population response to manipulation in southern Utah. Wildlife Society Bulletin 20:224-227.

Little, S. J., R. G. Harcourt, and A. P. Clevenger. 2002. Do wildlife passages act as prey-traps? Biological Conservation 107:135-145.

Litvaitis, J. A., K. Titus, and E. M. Anderson. 1994. Measuring vertebrate use of terrestrial habitats and foods. Pages 254-174 in T. A. Bookhout, editor. Research and Management Techniques for Wildlife and Habitats. The Wildlife Society, Bethesda, Maryland, USA.

Logan, K. A. 1983. Mountain lion population and habitat characteristics in the Big Horn Mountains of Wyoming. Thesis, University of Wyoming, Laramie, Wyoming, USA.

_____, L. L. Irwin, and R. Skinner. 1986. Characteristics of a hunted mountain lion population in Wyoming. Journal of Wildlife Management 50:648-654.

_____, and L. L. Sweanor. 2000. Puma. Pages 347-377, in S. Demarias and P. Krausman, editors. Ecology and Management of Large Mammals in North America. Prentice Hall, Upper Saddle River, New Jersey, USA.

_____, and L. L. Irwin. 1985. Mountain lion habitats in the Big Horn Mountains, Wyoming. Wildlife Society Bulletin 13:257-262.

_____, and L. L. Sweanor. 2001. Desert Puma: Evolutionary Ecology and Conservation of an Enduring Carnivore. Island Press, Washington, D. C., USA.

_____, E. T. Thorne, L. L. Irwin, and R. Skinner. 1986. Immobilizing wild mountain lions (Felis concolor) with ketamine hydrochloride and xylazine hydrochloride. Journal of Wildlife Diseases 22:97-103.

_____, L. L. Sweanor, J. F. Smith, and M. G. Hornocker. 1999. Capturing pumas with foot-hold snares. Wildlife Society Bulletin 27:201-208.

_____, _____, and M. G. Hornocker. 2003. Reconciling science and politics in puma management in the West: New Mexico as a template. Proceedings of the Sixty-ninth North American Wildlife and Natural Resources Conference, Spokane, Washington, USA.

Longland, W. S., and M. V. Price. 1991. Direct observations of owls and heteromyid rodents: can predation risk explain microhabitat use? Ecology 72:2261-2273.

Lopez-Gonzalez, C. A. 1999. Implicaciones para la conservacion y el manejo de pumas (Puma concolor) utilizando como modelo una poblacion sugeta a caceria deportiva. Dissertation, Universidad Nacional Autonoma de Mexico.

Loxterman, J. L. 2001. The impact of habitat fragmentation on the population genetic structure of pumas in Idaho. Dissertation, Idaho State University, Pocatello, Idaho, USA.

Ludwig, D. 1999. Is it meaningful to estimate a probability of extinction? Ecology 80:298-310.

MacArthur, R. H. 1972. Geographical ecology: patterns in the distribution of species. Harper and Row, New York, New York, USA.

Maehr, D. S., and G. B. Caddick. 1995. Demographics and genetic introgression in the Florida panther. Conservation Biology 9:1295-1298.

_____, E. D. Land, and J. C. Roof. 1991. Social ecology of Florida panthers. National Geographic Research & Exploration 7:414-431.

_____, _____, D. B. Shindle, O. L. Bass, and T. S. Hoctor. 2002. Florida panther dispersal and conservation. Biological Conservation 106:187-197.

_____, J. C. Roof, E. D. Land, and J. W. McCown. 1989. First reproduction of a panther (*Felis concolor coryi*) in southwestern Florida, U.S.A. Mammalia 53:129-131.

Mahoney, S. P., and J. A. Schaefer. 2002. Long-term changes in demography and migration of Newfoundland caribou. Journal of Mammalogy 83:957-963.

Mangus, G. 1991. Legal aspects of encounters on federal lands and in state programs. Pages 86-94 *in* C. S. Braun, editor. Cougar-human interaction symposium and workshop, Colorado Division of Wildlife, Denver, Colorado, USA.

Mattson, D. J., J. V. Hart, P. Beier, and J. Millen-Johnson. 2003. A conceptual model and appraisal of existing research related to interactions between humans and pumas. Abstract, Proceedings of the Seventh Cougar Workshop, Jackson, Wyoming, USA.

Martorello, D. A. and R. A. Beausoleil. 2003. Cougar harvest characteristics with and without the use of hounds. Abstract, Seventh Mountain Lion Workshop, Jackson, Wyoming, USA.

Mazzoli, M. 2003. Relationships between land tenure system, mountain lion protection status, and livestock depredation rate. Proceedings of the Seventh Mountain Lion Workshop, Jackson Hole, Wyoming, USA. In press.

McBride, R. T. 2001. Current panther distribution, population trends, and habitat use: a review of field work fall 2000-winter 2001. Unpublished Report to Florida panther subteam of MERIT, U.S. Fish and Wildlife Service, Vero Beach, Florida, USA.

_____. 2002. Florida panther current verified population, distribution, and highlights of field work fall 2001-winter 2002. Unpublished Report to Florida panther subteam of MERIT, U.S. Fish and Wildlife Service, Vero Beach, Florida, USA.

McCullough, D. R. 1979. The George Reserve deer herd: population ecology of a K-selected species. The University of Michigan Press, Ann Arbor, Michigan, USA.

McDaniel, G. W., K. S. McKelvey, J. R. Squires, and L. Ruggiero. 2000. Efficacy of lures and hair snares to detect lynx. Wildlife Society Bulletin 28:119-123.

McRae, B. H. 2004. Integrating landscape ecology and population genetics: conventional tools and a new model. Dissertation, Northern Arizona University, Flagstaff, Arizona, USA.

Mduma, S. A. R., A. R. E. Sinclair, and R. Hilborn. 1999. Food regulates the Serengeti wildebeest: a 40-year record. Journal of Animal Ecology 68:1101-1122.

Meffe, G. K. and C. R. Carroll, editors. 1997. Principles of conservation biology. 2nd edition. Sinauer Associates, Sunderland, Massachusetts, USA.

Meinke, C. W. 2004. Mountain lion habitat use relative to human activity in the Redwood Creek Basin of northwest California. Thesis, Humboldt State University, Arcata, California, USA.

Messier, F. 1994. Ungulate population models with predation: a case study with the North American moose. Ecology 75:478-488.

Mihan, R. Department of the Interior. Solicitor. Oakland, California, USA.

Minnis, D. L. 1998. Wildlife-policy making by the electorate: an overview of citizen-sponsored ballot measures on hunting and trapping. Wildlife Society Bulletin 26:75-83.

Minta, S. C., P. M. Kareiva, and A. P. Curlee. 1999. Carnivore research and conservation: learning from history and theory. Pages 323-404, *in* T. W. Clark, A. P. Curlee, S. C. Minta, and P. M. Kareiva, editors. Carnivores in ecosystems: the Yellowstone experience. Yale University Press, New Haven, Connecticut, USA.

Moorhead, B., and T. Hofstra. 1995. Western park personnel meet on cougar-human encounters. Park Science Fall, 1994, 14(4) 20-21.

Mowat, G., and C. Strobeck. 2000. Estimating population size of grizzly bears using hair capture, DNA profiling and mark-recapture analysis. Journal of Wildlife Management 64:183-93.

Murphy, K. 1983. Characteristics of a hunted population of mountain lions in Western Montana. Final job report. Project W-120-R-13 and 14.

Murphy, K. M. 1998. The ecology of the cougar (*Puma concolor*) in the northern Yellowstone ecosystem: interactions with prey, bears, and humans. Dissertation, University of Idaho, Moscow, Idaho, USA.

Murtaugh, P. A. 2002. On rejection rates of paired intervention analysis. Ecology 83:1752-1761.

Noss, R., and J. M. Scott. 1997. Ecosystem protection and restoration: the core of ecosystem management. Pages 239-264 *in* M.S. Boyce and A. Haney, editors. Ecosystem Management: Applications for Sustainable Forest and Wildlife Resources. Yale University Press, New Haven, Connecticut, USA.

Noss, R. F. 1991 From endangered species to biodiversity. Pages 227-246 *in* K. A. Kohm, editor. Balancing on the brink of extinction: The Endangered Species Act and lessons for the future. Island Press, Washington, D.C., USA.

Nowak, M. C. 1999. Predation rates and foraging ecology of adult female mountain lions in northeastern Oregon. Thesis, Washington State University, Pullman, Washington, USA.

Nowak, R. M. 1976. The cougar in the United States and Canada. U. S. Department of the Interior, Fish and Wildlife Service, Washington D.C., and New York Zoological Society, New York, USA.

Paine, R. T. 1974. Intertidal community structure: experimental studies on the relationship between a dominant competitor and its principal predator. Oecologia 15: 93-120.

Peek, J. M. 1986. A Review of Wildlife Management. Prentice-Hall, New Jersey, USA.

Pierce, B. M. and V. C. Bleich. 2003. Mountain Lion. Pages 744-757 in G. A. Feldhamer, B. C. Thompson, and J. A. Chapman, editors. Wild mammals of North America: biology, management, and conservation, 2nd edition. The Johns Hopkins University Press, Baltimore, Maryland, USA.

_____, W. S. Longland, and S. H. Jenkins. 1992. Rattlesnake predation on desert rodents: microhabitat and species-specific effects on risk. Journal of Mammalogy 73:859-865.

_____, V. C. Bleich, and R. T. Bowyer. 1999. Population dynamics of mountain lions and mule deer: top-down or bottom-up regulation? Final report. Deer Herd Management Plan Implementation Program, California Department of Fish and Game, Sacramento, California, USA.

_____, _____, and _____. 2000a. Selection of mule deer by mountain lions and coyotes: effects of hunting style, body size, and reproductive status. Journal of Mammalogy 81:462-472.

_____, _____, and _____. 2000b. Social organization of mountain lions: does a land-tenure system regulate population size? Ecology 81:1533-1543.

_____, _____, C. L. B. Chetkiewicz, and J. D. Wehausen. 1998. Timing of feeding bouts of mountain lions. Journal of Mammalogy 79:222-226.

_____, _____, J. D. Wehausen, and R. T. Bowyer. 1999b. Migratory patterns of mountain lions: implications for social regulation and conservation. Journal of Mammalogy 80:986-992.

Pollock, K. H., S. R. Winterstein, C. M. Bunck, and P. D. Curtis. 1989. Survival analysis in telemetry studies: the staggered entry design. Journal of Wildlife Management 53:7-15.

Polo, M., and R. Latham. 1958. The travels of Marco Polo. Penguin Books, London.

Rachlow, J. L., and J. Berger. 1998. Reproduction and population density: trade-offs for the conservation of rhinos in situ. Animal Conservation 1:101-106.

Ratti, J. T, and E. O. Garton. 1994. Research and experimental design. Pages 1-23 in T. A. Bookhout, editor. Research and Management Techniques for Wildlife and Habitat. Fifth edition. The Wildlife Society, Bethesda, Maryland, USA.

Redwood National and State Parks. 1995. Standard operating procedures (SOP): reporting and responding to cougar observations in Redwood National and State Parks. Unpublished file report. Redwood National Park, Orick, California, USA.

Riley, S. J. 1998. Integration of environmental, biological, and human dimensions for management of mountain lions (*Puma concolor*) in Montana. Dissertation, Cornell University, Ithaca, New York, USA.

Robinette, W. L., J. S. Gashwiler, and O. W. Morris. 1959. Food habits of the cougar in Utah and Nevada. Journal Wildlife Management 23:261-273.

_____, _____, and _____. 1961. Notes on cougar productivity and life history. Journal of Mammalogy 42:204-217.

Roelke, M. E., J. S. Martenson, and S. J. O'Brien. 1993. The consequences of demographic reduction and genetic depletion in the endangered Florida panther. Current Biology 3:340-350.

Ross, P. I, and M. G. Jalkotzy. 1996. Cougar predation on moose in south-western Alberta. Alces 32:1-8.

_____, _____, and M. Festa-Bianchet. 1997. Cougar predation on bighorn sheep in southwestern Alberta during winter. Canadian Journal of Zoology 74:771-775.

_____, and M. G. Jalkotzy. 1992. Characteristics of a hunted population of cougars in southwestern Alberta. Journal of Wildlife Management 56:417-426.

_____, _____, and P. Daoust. 1995. Fatal traumas sustained by cougars while attacking prey in southern Alberta. Canadian Field-Naturalist 109:261-263.

Roy, L. D., and M. J. Dorrance. 1976. Methods of investigating predation on domestic livestock: a manual for investigating officers. Alberta Agriculture, Plant Industry Laboratory, Alberta, Canada.

Ruth, T. K. 1991. Cougar use in an area of high recreational development in Big Bend National Park, Texas. Thesis, Texas A&M University, College Station, Texas, USA.

Ruth, T. K., K. A. Logan, L. L. Sweanor, M. G. Hornocker, and L. J. Temple. 1998. Evaluating cougar translocation in New Mexico. Journal of Wildlife Management 62:1264-1275.

_____. 2001. Cougar-Wolf interactions in Yellowstone National Park: competition, demographics, and spatial relationships. June 2001 Annual Technical Report, Wildlife Conservation Society/Hornocker Wildlife Institute.

_____, K. M. Murhpy, and P. C. Buotte. 2003. Presence and movements of lactating and maternal female cougars: implications for state hunting regulations. Proceedings to the Seventh Mountain Lion Workshop, Jackson, Wyoming, USA.

Sams, M. G., R. L. Lockmiller, C. W. Qualls, Jr., D. M. Leslie, Jr., and M. E. Payton. 1996. Physiological correlates of neonatal mortality in an overpopulated herd of white-tailed deer. Journal of Mammalogy 77:179-190.

Sawyer, H. and F. Lindzey. 2002. A Review of predation on bighorn sheep (*Ovis canadensis*). Wyoming Cooperative Fish and Wildlife Research Unit, Laramie, Wyoming, USA.

Schaefer, R. J., S. G. Torres, and V. C. Bleich. 2000. Survivorship and cause-specific mortality in sympatric populations of mountain sheep and mule deer. California Fish and Game 86:127-135.

Seidensticker, J. C., IV, M. G. Hornocker, W. V. Wiles, and J. P. Messick. 1973. Mountain lion social organization in the Idaho primitive area. Wildlife Monograph 35:1-60.

Shaw, H. G. 1977. Impact of mountain lion on mule deer and cattle in northwestern Arizona. Pages 17-32 in R. L. Phillips, and C. J. Jonkel, editors. Proceedings of the 1975 predator symposium. Montana Forest and Conservation Experiment Station, University of Montana, Missoula, Montana, USA.

_____. 1980. Ecology of the mountain lion in Arizona. Final report, P-R Project W-78-R, Work Plan 2, Job 13. Arizona Game and Fish Department, Phoenix, Arizona, USA.

_____. 1983. Mountain lion field guide. Special Report Number 9 Arizona Game and Fish Department, Phoenix, Arizona, USA.

Shindle, D., D. Land, M. Cunningham, and M. Lotz. 2001. Florida panther genetic restoration. Annual Report 2000-01. Florida Fish and Wildlife Conservation Commission, Tallahassee, Florida, USA.

Shinn, K. J. 2002. Ocelot distribution in the Lower Rio Grande Valley National Wildlife Refuge. Unpublished thesis, University of Texas-Pan American, Edinburg, Texas, USA.

Simberloff, D., J. A. Farr, J. Cox, and D. W. Mehlman. 1992. Movement corridors: conservation bargains or poor investments? Conservation Biology 6:493-504.

Sinclair, E. A., E. L. Swenson, M. L. Wolfe, D. C. Choate, B. Gates, and K. A. Crandall. 2001. Gene flow estimates in Utah cougars imply management beyond Utah. Animal Conservation 4:257-264.

Singer, F. J., A. Harting, K. K. Symonds, and M. B. Coughenour. 1997. Density dependence, compensation, and environmental effects on elk calf mortality in Yellowstone National Park. Journal of Wildlife Management 61:12-25.

Skogland, T. 1990. Density dependence in a fluctuating wild reindeer herd; maternal vs. offspring effects. Oecologia 84:442-450.

Smallwood, K. S. 1997. Interpreting puma (*Puma concolor*) population estimates for theory and management. Environmental Conservation 24:283-289.

_____, and E. L. Fitzhugh. 1995. A track count for estimating mountain lion population trend. Biological Conservation 71:251-259.

Smith, T. E., R. R. Duke, M. J. Kutilek, and H. T. Harvey. 1986. Mountain lions (*Felis concolor*) in the vicinity of Carlsbad Caverns National Park, New Mexico, and Guadalupe Mountains National Park, Texas. Final Report. U.S. Department of Interior, National Park Service, Santa Fe, New Mexico, USA.

Soulé, M. E. 1985. What is conservation biology? Bioscience 35:19-40.

_____, J. Estes, J. Berger, C. Martinez. 2003. Ecological effectiveness: conservation goals for interactive species. Conservation Biology 17:1238-1250.

Spalding, D. J., and J. Lesowski. 1971. Winter food of the cougar in south-central British Columbia. Journal of Wildlife Management 35:378-381.

Starfield, A. M., and A. L. Bleloch. 1986. Building models for conservation and wildlife management. Macmillan, New York, New York, USA.

Stewart-Oaten, A., and J. R. Bence. 2001. Temporal and spatial variation in environmental impact assessment. Ecological Monographs 71:305-339.

_____, and W. W. Murdoch. 1986. Environmental impact assessment: 'pseudoreplication' in time? Ecology 67:929-940.

Stoner, D. C. 2004. Cougar exploitation levels in Utah: Implications for demographic structure, metapopulation dynamics, and population recovery. Thesis, Utah State University, Logan, Utah, USA.

_____. and M.L. Wolf. 2003. Defining and delineating De Facto refugia: a preliminary analysis of the spatial distribution of cougar harvest in Utah and implications for conservation. Abstract. Seventh Mountain Lion Workshop, Jackson Hole, Wyoming, USA.

Suttie, J. M., and R. N. B. Kay. 1983. The influence of nutrition and photoperiod on the growth of antlers of young red deer. Pages 61-71 in R. D. Brown, editor. Antler development in Cervidae. Caesar Kleberg Wildlife Research Institute, Kingsville, Texas, USA.

Sweanor, L. L., K. A. Logan, M. G. Hornocker. Cougar responses to close encounters with researchers. Wildlife Society Bulletin. In press.

_____, _____, and _____. 2000. Cougar dispersal patterns, metapopulation dynamics and conservation. Conservation Biology 13:798-808.

Sweitzer, R. A., S. H. Jenkins, and J. Berger. 1997. Near-extinction of porcupine by mountain lions and consequences of ecosystem change in the Great Basin Desert. Conservation Biology 6:1407-1417.

Swihart, R. K., H. P. Weeks Jr., A. L. Easter-Pilcher, and A. J. DeNicola. 1998. Nutritional condition and fertility of white-tailed deer (*Odocoileus virginianus*) from areas with contrasting histories of hunting. Canadian Journal of Zoology 76:1932-1941.

Teel, T. L., R. S. Krannich, and R. H. Schmidt. 2002. Utah stakeholders' attitudes toward selected cougar and black bear management practices. Wildlife Society Bulletin 30:2-15.

Terborgh, J., J. A. Estes, P. Paquet, K. Ralls, D. Boyd-Hager, B. J. Miller, and R. F. Noss. 1999. The role of top carnivores in regulating terrestrial ecosystems. Pages 39-64 in Soulé, M. E. and J. Terborgh, editors. Continental Conservations. Island Press, Washington D.C., USA.

Torres, S. G. 2004. Lion Sense. The Globe Pequot Press, Guilford, Connecticut, USA.

_____, H. Keough, D. Dawn. 2004. Puma management in western North America: a 100 year retrospective. Presented at Seventh Mountain Lion Workshop, Jackson Hole, Wyoming, USA. In prep.

_____, and T. Lupo. 2000. Statewide model helps biologists understand mountain lions' habitat loss. Outdoor California. May/June:22-23.

_____, T. M. Mansfield, J. E. Foley, T. Lupo, and A. Brinkhaus. 1996. Mountain lion and human activity in California: testing speculations. Wildlife Society Bulletin 24:451-460.

Trolle, M., and M. Kery. 2003. Estimation of ocelot density in the Pantanal using capture-recapture analysis of camera-trapping data. Journal of Mammalogy 84:607-614.

Turner J. W. Jr., M. L. Wolfe, and J. F. Kirkpatrick. 1992. Seasonal mountain lion predation on a feral horse population. Canadian Journal of Zoology 70:929-934.

Ullrey, D. E. 1983. Nutrition and antler development in white-tailed deer. Pages 49-59 in R. D. Brown, editor. Antler Development in Cervidae. Caesar Kleberg Wildlife Research Institute, Kingsville, Texas, USA.

Underwood, A. J. 1992. Beyond BACI: The detection of environmental impacts on populations in the real, but variable, world. Journal of Experimental Marine Biology and Ecology 161:145-178.

_____. 1994. On beyond BACI: Sampling designs that might reliably detect environmental disturbances. Ecological Applications 4:3-15.

[USDT] U.S. Department of Transportation. 2004. Traffic safety facts 2002: a compilation of motor vehicle crash data from the Fatality Analysis Reporting System and the General Estimates System. National Highway Traffic Safety Administration, Washington D.C., USA.

Van Sickle, W. D., and F. G. Lindzey. 1991. Evaluation of a cougar population estimator based on probability sampling. Journal of Wildlife Management 55:738-743.

Wachter, B., O. I. Hoener, M. I. Mast, W. Golla, and H. Hofer. 2002. Low aggression levels and unbiased sex ratios in a prey-rich environment: no evidence of siblicide in Ngorongoro spotted hyenas (Crocuta crocuta). Behavioral Ecology and Sociobiology 52:348-356.

Wade, D.A., and J. E. Bowns. 1982. Procedures on evaluating predation on livestock and wildlife. Texas A&M University (Texas Agricultural Extension Service, The Texas Agriculture Experiment Station), U.S. Fish and Wildlife Service.

Walker, C. W., L. A. Harveson, M. T. Pittman, M. E. Tewes, and R. L. Honeycutt. 2000. Microsatellite variation in two populations of mountain lions in Texas. Southwestern Naturalist 45:196-203.

Wehausen, J. D. 1996. Effects of mountain lion predation on bighorn sheep in the Sierra Nevada and Granite Mountains of California. Wildlife Society Bulletin 24:471-479.

White, G. C., A. B. Franklin, and T. M. Shenk. 2002. Estimating parameters of PVA models from data on marked animals. Pages 169-190 in S. R. Beissinger and D. R. McCullough, editors. Population viability analysis. University of Chicago Press, Chicago, Illinois, USA.

White, P. A., and D. K. Boyd. 1989. A cougar, Felis concolor, kitten killed and eaten by gray wolves, Canis lupus, in Glacier National Park, Montana. Canadian Field-Naturalist 103:408-409.

Whittaker, D. G., and S. G. Torres. 1998. Ballot initiatives and natural resource management: some opinions on processes, impacts, and experience. Human Dimensions of Wildlife 3(2)1-7.

Williams, B. K., J. D. Nichols, and M. J. Conroy. 2002. Analysis and management of animal populations. Academic Press, New York, New York, USA.

Young, S. P. and E. A. Goldman. 1946. The puma: mysterious American cat. The American Wildlife Institute, Washington D.C., USA.

Zinn, H. C., and M. J. Manfredo. 1996. Societal preferences for mountain lion management along Colorado's front range. Human Dimensions in Natural Resources Unit, College of Natural Resources, Colorado State University, Fort Collins, Colorado, USA.

The *Cougar Management Guidelines* are available for $21.95 U.S./ $28.95 Canadian, including shipping and handling. Contact for quantity discounts.

Ordering Options:
Phone: (866) 375-9015
Email: orders@opalcreekpress.com
Fax: 503-363-6228
Mail: Opal Creek Press, LLC
       1675 Fir Street S.
       Salem, OR 97302

WildFutures
Bainbridge Island, Washington

The text for this book is printed on 100% post-consumer chlorine free New Leaf paper.
The cover is printed on 15% post-consumer fiber.